Henry Norton

Deeds of Daring

History of the Eighth New York Volunteer Cavalry

Henry Norton

Deeds of Daring

History of the Eighth New York Volunteer Cavalry

ISBN/EAN: 9783337813468

Printed in Europe, USA, Canada, Australia, Japan

Cover: Foto ©ninafisch / pixelio.de

More available books at **www.hansebooks.com**

DEEDS OF DARING,

OR

HISTORY OF THE EIGHTH

N. Y. VOLUNTEER CAVALRY,

CONTAINING A COMPLETE RECORD OF THE
BATTLES, SKIRMISHES, MARCHES, ETC., THAT
THE GALLANT EIGHTH NEW YORK CAVALRY
PARTICIPATED IN, FROM ITS ORGAN-
IZATION IN NOVEMBER, 1861, TO THE
CLOSE OF THE REBELLION
IN 1865.

Compiled and Edited by

HENRY NORTON,

NORWICH, N. Y.:
CHENANGO TELEGRAPH PRINTING HOUSE,
1889.

TO THE
OFFICERS AND MEMBERS
OF THE
EIGHTH NEW YORK VOLUNTEER CAVALRY,

AND THE VETERAN VOLUNTEERS OF MONROE, ONTARIO, SENECA, WAYNE, ORLEANS, NIAGARA, CHENANGO, AND ONEIDA COUNTIES,
AND
THE EIGHTH ILLINOIS, THIRD INDIANA, TWELFTH ILLINOIS, FIRST VERMONT, FIRST NEW HAMPSHIRE, TWENTY-SECOND NEW YORK AND FIFTEENTH NEW YORK CAVALRY, THAT THE EIGHTH NEW YORK CAVALRY ASSOCIATED WITH IN THE WAR OF THE REBELLION, THIS VOLUME IS DEDICATED BY
THE AUTHOR

HENRY NORTON.

February, 1889.

CONTENTS.

CHAPTER I.

Enlisting in Chenango county in '61—The Chenango county boys' trip to Rochester—First night at Rochester—First soldiers' meal—Sworn in—Consolidation—Camp duty—Muster in of the regiment—The trip to Washington, D. C—Camp Selden—Camp duty—Drilling—Winter weather—Sickness and death.

CHAPTER II.

Picket duty on the Ohio and Chesapeake canal—Harper's Ferry—Charlestown—Picket duty on the Potomac and Winchester railroad—The battle of Winchester, May, '62—The Eighth New York Cavalry on foot—A great skedaddle—The exploits of the prisoners, taken in that battle, in rebel prison, as told by one of the survivors—Maryland Heights—Marching around the country on foot—Relay house—Colonel Davis—Drawing horses—Drilling horses—Back to Harper's Ferry again—Scouting—Surrounded.

CHAPTER III.

The escape of the cavalry—Going through rebel General Longstreet's corps—Capture of a rebel wagon train—The good people of Green Castle—Battle of Antietam—The rebels' retreat—The Eighth New York Cavalry crossing and re-crossing the Potomac river—In camp at Haggerstown—Crossing the Potomac river into Virginia—The great march to Fredericksburg—Snicker's Gap—The engagements of Philamont, Union, Upperville, Barber's Crossroads, Amosville, Jefferson and Sulphur Springs come in rapid succession—Great counter-charge at Barber's Crossroads—Retreat of the rebels to the mountains—

Supper on fresh beef alone—Charge of the bee-hives—The artillery duel—The arrival at Fredericksburg—On picket at Bank's Ford, on the Rappahannock river—Trading with rebel pickets—Foraging—Hoe cake—On picket in King George's county—The battle of Fredericksburg.

CHAPTER IV.

Building winter quarters—Short stay—Burnside's strategy—Building fires—Burnside stuck in the mud—Stafford Court House—Picketing at Dumfries—Guerrillas—Bushwhackers—Snow—Cold weather.

CHAPTER V.

The cavalry on the move—Skirmishing—Foraging—Crossing the Rapidan—Battle of Chancellorsville—Recrossing the river—In camp—The march to Beverly Ford—The battle of Beverly Ford—Death of General Davis, Captain Foote and Lieutenant Cutler—Lee's invasion—A great march—Fight at Middleburg—Crossing the Potomac river into Maryland again—The march to Gettysburg—The battle of Gettysburg.

CHAPTER VI.

The rebels retreat—The cavalry on the move—Skirmishing—Fight at Funkstown—Capture of a rebel gun—Across the Potomac river into Virginia again—Travelling the same ground over again—Rappahannock Station—On picket—Germania Ford—Madison Court House—Brandy Station—Culpepper—Kelly's Ford—Driving the rebels south of Rapidan—Winter quarters—The Eighth New York Cavalry's transfer to the Second Brigade, Third Division, April, '64—Crossing the Rapidan—The raid to Richmond, May, '64—Grant's flank movement—White House Landing—Malvern Hill—James river—Petersburg—The Wilson raid in June, '64.

CHAPTER VII.

Rebel prison—Sanitary commission—Picket—Prince George Court House—Springing of mines—City Point—Transferred to the Shenandoah Valley—Guarding a wagon train—Hallstown—Into Maryland again—Across the Potomac river into Virginia—At Shepardstown Ford—Scouting.

CHAPTER VIII.

Opequan Creek—Mosby—Surprised at Snicker's Gap, '64—Battle of Winchester in '64—Chester Gap—Skirmishing—Millford—Newmarket Gap—Harrisburg—Staunton—General Custer—Paid off—Drawing rations—Mill Creek—Columbia Furnace—Cedar Creek—The battle of Cedar Creek.

CHAPTER IX.

Picket duty—Scouting—Fisher's Hill—Retreat—Reconnoissance by moonlight—Mount Jackson—Winter weather—Crossing Cedar Creek—Foraging—Reconnoitering—Woodstock—The rebels charge on our brigade—Driving the rebels back—Christmas—Good news from Sherman's army—Winter quarters—Execution of two deserters belonging to the Third New York Cavalry—Exploits of a cavalryman in camp—Skirmishing—On the march—Waynesboro—Charging the rebels' breastworks—A great feat—Rebel General Early—Rebel prisoners—Tye river—Burning railroad bridges.

CHAPTER X.

Buffalo river—Scottsville—Columbia—Frederick's Hall—Beaver Dam Station—South Anna—North Anna—Matapony—Pamunkey river—Five Forks—The cavalry charge—South Side railroad—Capture of Richmond—Appomattox Station—Flag of truce—Close of the war—General Custer's remarks—Trip to Washington—Grand review—Post of honor—Custer's compliment—Custer's farewell—Back into Virginia again—Drilling—Homeward bound—The final discharge.

APPENDIX.

Roster of the Regiment—Promotions—List of the killed, wounded, prisoners, died of wounds, died in rebel prisons, died of disease, the postoffice address of survivors.

PREFACE.

THE author has written this History of the Eighth New York Cavalry for the interests of officers and members of the Regiment, and the veteran volunteers of Monroe, Ontario, Seneca, Wayne, Orleans, Niagara, Chenango and Oneida counties; and of all veterans of the war, their kindred and friends, and those who sympathize with the men who fought for the Union.

At the urgent request of such comrades, their kindred and friends, the author has written this History of the gallant Eighth New York Cavalry, being a complete record of the Regiment, from its organization in November, 1861, to the close of the Rebellion, in 1865. The author has taken ample time to collect facts and official records; also he has received many communications from comrades of the Regiment.

He believes the book will be highly appreciated in every family of Monroe, Ontario, Seneca, Wayne, Orleans, Niagara, Chenango and Oneida counties, for the soldiers of the Eighth New York Cavalry were, some of them, kindred or friends to them.

The author has endeavored to truthfully describe the scenes of army life and the incidents which occurred in the ranks of the Eighth New York Cavalry.

Accurate dates are given in recounting journeys, marches, battles, skirmishes, the picket line, camp life, prison pen, hair-breadth escapes, etc., etc.

The author has spared no pains or expense to make the History a success. His wish is that the comrades will extend the circulation of this book, and see that all of their kindred and friends are supplied with a copy. I remain,

Yours in F., C. & L.,

NORWICH, N. Y., 1889.   HENRY NORTON.

DEEDS OF DARING, OR HISTORY OF THE EIGHTH N. Y. VOLUNTEER CAVALRY.

CHAPTER I.

ENLISTING IN CHENANGO COUNTY IN '61—THE CHENANGO COUNTY BOYS' TRIP TO ROCHESTER—FIRST NIGHT AT ROCHESTER—FIRST SOLDIERS' MEAL—SWORN IN—CONSOLIDATION—CAMP DUTY—MUSTER IN OF THE REGIMENT—THE TRIP TO WASHINGTON, D. C.—CAMP SELDEN—CAMP DUTY—DRILLING—WINTER WEATHER—SICKNESS AND DEATH.

THE Eighth New York Volunteer Cavalry was organized at Rochester, N. Y., and mustered into the United States service November 28th, 1861, for three years.

Through the summer of 1861, Alfred S. Kinney, of Sherburne, Chenango county, N. Y., undertook to enlist a company of men for a cavalry regiment. It ran along until October. Kinney had only thirty-four men enlisted. In October he was ordered on with what men he had. There were forty men who went from Chenango county in '61 and joined the Eighth New York Cavalry.

After we reached Rochester and were sworn into the United States service, Walter B. Norton returned to Chenango, on leave of absence, and recruited enough more men to make the forty.

On the 21st of October, 1861, Kinney, with his

men, started from Norwich, N. Y. We had to go with wagons from that place to Utica. There was no railroad through the Chenango valley at that time. On the morning of the 21st we started from Norwich in two wagons, arriving at Sherburne a little before noon, we made a halt at that place to take on more men. After everything was ready, we started again in the afternoon for Utica. The boys had a jolly time. They were singing, laughing and joking all the way along.

At that time, there was a plank road through the valley and a toll gate every four or five miles. The boys would get out of the wagons every little while to see what they could find. There were corn fields close to the road, and the boys would go for the pumpkins. They would carry two or three with them to the wagons. When the teams would come along to the toll gate, and when they were paying toll, the gate keeper would almost always leave the door open. The boys would take one of the pumpkins and let it drive with all of their might into the house, and would say:

"Old man, you may have that to make pumpkin pies with."

We did not go any farther than Oriskany Falls the first day. We arrived there about sundown, ate our suppers and went out to see the town. When we came to go to bed, it was like a batch of hop-pickers. Some would not sleep, and they let none of the others sleep. We arose in the morning, ate our breakfast and started again. We arrived in

Utica before noon, and stayed there until about the middle of the afternoon, when we took the cars for Rochester.

We arrived at our destination just at dark. The camp was situated on the outskirts of the city. They had barracks built for the men. Companies A, B, C, D, E, F and G were organized and already there. The nights were quite cool at that time of the year. There were coal stoves in the barracks, and bunks, built three tiers high. We had blankets dealt out to us, and had to get along the best we could until morning. I had heard of people sleeping on the soft side of a plank, but I slept on the soft side of a board that night. There was not much sleep for the boys that night; some of them stayed close to the stove. I think some of them did not lie down that night.

William Sage, Walter B. Norton, Milo Church, and several others were sitting around the stove talking. Their conversation ran in the direction of the war. William Sage said: "Boys, I don't believe that we will be gone over six months. We can whip the 'rebs' out in that time."

One of the boys around the stove said: "I hope we will get down there before it is all over, I would like to get a whack at a 'reb' before the war closes."

The boys saw all the rebels they wanted. The war lasted three years, five months and seventeen days from that time.

In the morning, the first thing was to get ready for breakfast. They had men detailed to cook.

They would put two or three bushels of potatoes into a big kettle and cook them with skins on. They had a table made by driving posts into the ground and nailing boards on to them about three feet high. Every man had to stand up to eat. They had tin plates, tin cups, knives and forks. Each one got so much—two or three potatoes, a piece of meat, a chunk of bread and a cup of coffee, enough for a good meal. It went against the grain to have to eat off from a tin plate and to drink coffee out of a tin cup, with no milk in your coffee; and when I went to reach for the butter—there was none there. I probably never had eaten a meal without butter before. My appetite was poor that morning. I saw that all of the boys did not eat much, but never said anything. In less than thirteen months from that time, the boys would have given any amount of money, if they had it, for a meal no better than they had that morning at Rochester, that we stuck our noses up at. Not one of the boys of the Eighth New York had any idea what they had to go through, when they enlisted as soldiers.

The following are the names of the men who went from Chenango county in '61 into the Eighth:

William D. Adams.
George W. Atwell.
George W. Brooks.
Gilbert Brown.
Edward P. Beasley.
Stephen A. Barnes.
Nelson R. Brown.
Sidney M. Briggs.

Chauncey McIntyre.
Laguard Norton.
Henry Norton.
Albert Peck.
Edwin B. Paul.
George Rhoads.
David Shippey, Jr.
Albert Scott.

Philander Bowdish.
Milo Church.
John L. Church.
Benjamin L. Curtiss.
Joseph Edmonds.
Charles D. Geer.
Charles H. Graves.
William R. Guile.
William H. Howard.
Gilbert Harvey.
Riley Lowe.
Tennis L. Lowe.
Daniel D. Main.

Stephen D. Scott.
William Sage.
George B. Winsor.
Charles D. Follett.
Andrew M. Dickenson.
Edward A. Miner.
Walter B. Norton.
Enos Guile.
Jasper B. Cheney.
Alfred S. Kinney.
Israel Lynch.
Samuel Church.

There were quite a number who enlisted afterwards—in '62 and '63. Van B. Crain, of Norwich, recruited a squad of twenty men in '62, for the Eighth New York Cavalry. The men who went out in '61 were all young men, genuine yankees. Their forefathers fought in the Revolutionary War, and none braver than they went to the war.

When Alfred S. Kinney arrived at Rochester with his men, another man was in the same fix. George H. Barry, from Monroe county, had about the same number of men. They had to consolidate the two together and form one company. George H. Barry was elected Captain, Alfred S. Kinney, First Lieutenant, and Daniel E. Sackett, Second Lieutenant. That was Company H. Soon after that, Company I came from Oneida county. That was the ninth company. That was the extent of the regiment in '61.

There was not much going on from that time until we went to Washington. There was a camp guard around the camp to keep the boys in, and we used to have quite a time running the guard and going down town. Some of the boys had a leave of absence for a few days to go home again. It ran along until the first of December, when we had orders to move to Washington, D. C. We went via Elmira, and had a jolly time. Nothing of importance happened while going. We arrived safe and sound in a few days, and went into camp near Washington. The camp was called Camp Selden. We did camp duty, drilling and dress parade.

We drilled with the saber until we had it down to perfection. Every man was an expert with the saber. We did not draw horses until July, 1862. The government having cavalry enough at that time, there was talk that it was going to discharge the whole regiment, but we were kept in the service.

The change of climate caused a large amount of sickness the first winter at Washington. Quite a number died of the black measles and fevers.

CHAPTER II.

PICKET DUTY ON THE OHIO AND CHESAPEAKE CANAL—HARPER'S FERRY—CHARLESTOWN—PICKET DUTY ON THE POTOMAC AND WINCHESTER RAILROAD—THE BATTLE OF WINCHESTER, MAY '62—THE EIGHTH NEW YORK CAVALRY ON FOOT—A GREAT SKEDADDLE—THE EXPLOITS OF THE PRISONERS TAKEN IN THAT BATTLE IN REBEL PRISON, AS TOLD BY ONE OF THE SURVIVORS—MARYLAND HEIGHTS—MARCHING AROUND THE COUNTRY ON FOOT—RELAY HOUSE—COLONEL DAVIS—DRAWING HORSES—DRILLING HORSES—BACK TO HARPER'S FERRY AGAIN—SCOUTING—SURROUNDED.

WE left Camp Selden March 8, 1862, for Edward's Ferry. The regiment did picket duty on the Ohio and Chesapeake canal from Washington to Harper's Ferry until April 5th. March 12th, the regiment moved from Edward's Ferry to Muddy Branch; April 1st, moved from Muddy Branch to Poolville; April 6th, moved from Poolville to Harper's Ferry; April 12th, moved from Harper's Ferry to two miles above Charlestown; April 14th, moved to Cameron's Station, on the Potomac and Winchester railroad.

The regiment did picket duty from that time until May 24th, when we went to Winchester. On May 25, 1862, was fought the battle of Winchester. Gen. Banks had command of the Union Army and Gen. Stonewall Jackson was in command of the Rebel Army.

Some of the boys did not like to go into a battle on foot. They said that they enlisted for cavalry, and the government could not make them fight on foot. In consequence some took "French leave." Some of them came back under Abraham Lincoln's Proclamation in '63; a few never came back. It was proved, before the war was over, that when a man enlisted, he was a soldier. Then he belonged to Uncle Sam, who could put him anywhere he saw fit, but most always he was allowed to serve in the branch of service for which he enlisted. In '64 there were a number of heavy artillery regiments which were taken out of forts and put at the front.

On the 25th of May, the regiment marched to Winchester and was put in the fight. We were in the front and stayed until the last. Stonewall Jackson's army outnumbered ours. We were firing away at them the best we could with the old Hall's carbines, when Stonewall Jackson ordered his army to advance. They charged down on us, firing at the same time. The regiment was nearly surrounded before the order was given to retreat. This was in the streets of Winchester. When the order was given to get out of there, the rebels were close on to us. The rebels were yelling—"Surrender, you yankees!" The boys got out of there on the double quick. They never stopped until they arrived in bands at Williamsport, on the Potomac river. There were about twenty taken prisoners in the regiment. John L. Church, Nathan Bowen, Randall J. Beadle, Myron Gibbs, William Kuin and Charles G. Hampton were taken prisoners from Company H. John McFarlin, of Company H, was killed—the first man killed in the regiment.

The regiment remained at Williamsport until the 3d of June, when it started for Harper's Ferry, and arrived on Maryland Heights June 4th.

The exploits in rebel prisons of the men who were taken prisoners in the battle of Winchester, as told by John L. Church, one of the survivors:

"In May, 1862, our regiment, the Eighth New York Cavalry, was stationed along the railroad from Harper's Ferry toward Winchester, Va. We were only partially armed and were not yet mounted. On the 24th of May, '62, we were ordered to Winchester. About half of the regiment reported there, that night. Banks' army was retreating. We stayed in the town that night. In the morning, the town was nearly surrounded by Stonewall Jackson's army. Our little band was formed in the streets. No one seemed to know anything about us. General Banks' train had been going toward Harper's Ferry all night. Our whole army only numbered about five thousand men; while the rebel army was reported to be thirty thousand strong.

"There was not very much fighting that morning. General Banks had to retreat or be cut off completely. We stood in line in the street and could see our troops file into the same street, north of us, and march at double quick towards Harper's Ferry. At last our Colonel rode towards the south end of the town and saw the rebels coming in on the same street with us. He turned and waved his hand for us to march.

We then started after the army. It left our little band of men, on foot and poorly armed, at the rear of the whole army.

"The rebels planted some guns in the same street with us, and shelled us; and some of the citizens fired on us from their doors and windows as we marched by. John McFarlin, of Company H, was killed in the street. Most of their shells passed over our heads. When we reached the edge of town, the rebels were charging down on our left flank, and it looked as though we could never get through. Then we received orders to break ranks and get through if possible. We did so; and the most of us got through. There were a few taken prisoners at this point; and the rest that were taken were cut off between there and Harper's Ferry, a distance of forty miles. I was taken some time in the afternoon. Those who took me in treated us well and marched us back to Winchester that night.

"There were taken prisoners out of our regiment, Captain John W. Dickenson, of Company C, and nineteen men all told. Out of Company H were myself, Randall Beadle, William Kuin, Nathan Bowen, Myron Gibbs, Charles Hampton. Out of other companies were Charles Banty, Nathan Masters, James Evans, Odekirk, Wheat, and others whose names I do not now remember. All the arms we had, at that time, were sabers and some old condemned Hall's carbines.

"We were taken to Winchester and put into the

court yard and remained there a week. Captain Dickenson was paroled into the street. About all we had to eat, for the week we were there, was what Captain Dickenson bought of the citizens and brought to us. The guards allowed him to pass over what he bought, and we divided it between us.

"I tell you, he proved himself to be a true friend in time of need.

"Then General Fremont's army were on the move from the west of us to cut off Stonewall Jackson, and he began to retreat south, taking us with him. General Fremont crowded the rebels so close that they pushed us along almost night and day. We could hear them fighting only a mile or two in the rear of us, as we marched along.

"At every little village, they would march us through with their bands playing "Dixie," and halt us long enough for the people to come out to look us over, and talk war to us. The first question was—'What are you-uns fighting for?' and wanted to know where our horns were. They had heard that the yankees had horns. We told them that we had shed our horns, but that in a few hours, when General Fremont's boys came along, they would see some 'yanks' with horns on. The citizens were worse than their soldiers, a great deal more insulting, but our boys were as saucy as they were.

"There were about two thousand prisoners in all; seven hundred effective men, the rest taken out of hospitals; suttlers, citizens, etc. They drove us along like a flock of sheep, day after day, with scarcely a mouthful to eat. I believe I could have eaten all they gave me for a week at one meal. I have seen strong men march until they would drop like dead men. We would have to march on and leave them. Whether they lived or died we never knew. About the first they gave us to eat of any amount, they dealt out a quantity of flour, and to about twenty men a bake kettle. Nothing but cold water and flour! We were so near starved we could not wait for it to bake through. When we broke it up into nineteen pieces, the dough would string out; but I believe it tasted the best of anything I ever ate in my life.

"When we reached Harrisonburg, the rebels put us in the court house and yard for the night. They drove a wagon loaded with loaves of bread up to the fence and pitched them over into the crowd, just as you have seen men pitch pumpkins to cows.

"A few boys escaped by taking up a board and crawling under the judge's stand and staying there until General Fremont's army marched in there.

"We crossed the Blue Ridge mountains near Waynesboro. They took us to Lynchburg, put us in the old fair grounds and kept us there about a month, and then took us to Richmond. Three of us, myself, Nathan Masters and James Evans, were sick, and were put into Libby prison. The rest of our boys were put on Belle Isle. The fare we received there was a small piece of bread once a day; every day or two a small cup of pea or bean soup, and two or three times a week a piece of meat about one inch square, all cooked without salt. What the 'rebs' gave us to eat would set the boys into a diarrhœa. That and scurvy was the cause of most of the deaths there. They were carried out dead most every day. There were no windows in the prison, all taken out, and if a man put his head out, the guard would shoot at him. There was one man killed while I was there.

"Those of us who were in the prison were paroled the 7th of September, and those on the Island, I think, were paroled about a week later. I was placed on one of our transports at Aken's Landing. There were about six hundred of us paroled out of prison that day, and taken to Fort Delaware, situated on an island in Delaware Bay. There were one or two who died on the way.

"I was nothing but skin and bones, and had to walk with the help of a cane. I was put in the hospital at that place and kept there about three months, and was then sent to Parole Camp, at Annapolis, Maryland. I was exchanged and joined the regiment about the first of April, 1863, at Stafford Court House, Virginia. I think, and am quite sure, that all of our boys got through alive; but some were so badly used up that they did no more service, but were discharged. I recruited up enough so that I served my full time out, but have not got over my prison life and never expect to."

The regiment did duty on the fortifications on

Maryland Heights until June 23d, when the regiment started for Relay House in Maryland. We arrived there on the 24th. The regiment was sent there to draw horses and equipments. Colonel Crooks having previously resigned, Captain Benjamin F. Davis, of the regular army, was made Colonel of the Eighth New York Cavalry. He was a military man clear through, the right man in the right place. He was a strict disciplinarian, and brought the regiment down under the regular army regulations.

Some of the boys thought he was too severe with them. They said that no man could bring a volunteer regiment under regular army style with success. We will see, before we get through, how Davis came out. Previous to Davis' taking command the boys were put in the guard house for punishment. That suited them too well. There would sometimes be twenty-five in at one time. Colonel Davis' mode of punishment was to make a soldier carry a rail on his shoulder and walk a ring until he gave orders for him to stop.

The regiment received part of their horses July 8th, and the rest about the 20th. Then came drilling horses. The boys were glad of that, for they were getting tired of the other kind of soldiering. They had been marched around on foot about long enough. They enlisted for cavalry and they wanted to serve in that capacity. The regiment was so well drilled with the saber that after the regiment was organized we were as good a regiment as any of the regulars

It was said by Generals that the Eighth New York Cavalry was the best drilled regiment in the service in the saber exercise.

We drilled our horses every day until the 29th of August, when we were ordered to Harper's Ferry. We had our horses in good shape and ready for business. In a short time after we were mounted and clothed in good shape, you would not have known that it was the same regiment that had been straggling in bands around the country.

On the 29th day of August the regiment started for Harper's Ferry. We went by railroad, arriving at Harper's Ferry the next day, in good shape and ready to fight the rebels. We found the Twelfth Illinois Cavalry, a squadron of the First Maryland Cavalry and 6th squadron of the First Rhode Island Cavalry there. The regiment was sent up the Shenandoah river scouting about every day to Charlestown and Shepardstown, to ascertain the whereabouts of the rebel cavalry.

We had not been there long before we found out that we were surrounded by the rebels. Harper's Ferry is situated on the forks of the Potomac and Shenandoah rivers. Across the Potomac is Maryland Heights, where the Union Army had artillery planted and well fortified. Across the Shenandoah is Loudan Heights, in Virginia, where Stonewall Jackson had artillery planted. About the 12th of September they commenced to shell each other. The egiment was camped in the valley below. We could hear the shells go through the air. Stonewall Jackson would say to his men—"Be careful not to drop any shells down there in the hollow, for I want those horses."

CHAPTER III.

THE ESCAPE OF THE CAVALRY—GOING THROUGH REBEL GENERAL LONGSTREET'S CORPS—CAPTURE OF A REBEL WAGON TRAIN—THE GOOD PEOPLE OF GREEN CASTLE—BATTLE OF ANTIETAM—THE REBELS RETREAT—THE EIGHTH NEW YORK CAVALRY CROSSING AND RE-CROSSING THE POTOMAC RIVER—IN CAMP AT HAGERSTOWN—CROSSING THE POTOMAC RIVER INTO VIRGINIA—THE GREAT MARCH TO FREDERICKSBURG—SNICKER'S GAP—THE ENGAGEMENTS OF PHILAMONT, UNION, UPPERVILLE, BARBER'S CROSS ROADS, AMOSVILLE, JEFFERSON AND SULPHUR SPRINGS COME IN RAPID SUCCESSION—GREAT COUNTER-CHARGE AT BARBER'S CROSS ROADS—RETREAT OF THE REBELS TO THE MOUNTAIN—SUPPER ON FRESH BEEF ALONE—CHARGE OF THE BEE-HIVES—THE ARTILLERY DUEL—THE ARRIVAL AT FREDERICKSBURG—ON PICKET AT BANKS' FORD, ON THE RAPPAHANNOCK RIVER—TRADING WITH REBEL PICKETS—FORAGING—HOE CAKE—ON PICKET IN KING GEORGE'S COUNTY—THE BATTLE OF FREDERICKSBURG.

ALL this time Colonel Davis was busy, for he was going to take his regiment out of Harper's Ferry, and not stay there and be gobbled up by the rebels without making an effort to get away. Colonel Davis found out when the rebels would take the Ferry. The rebels knew they could take it in short order when they got ready to make the attack.

The Colonel made preparations to go out the night before, with his regiment and what cavalry remained there. He got one of the old settlers, a man who had lived there all his life and knew the country well, to pilot him through Maryland, which was then occupied by rebel General Longstreet and his corps. He had a scout there to watch his movements, for he knew the only way to get out was to go through General Longstreet's corps.

On the 14th of September, everything was in readiness for us to get out of the Ferry, if we could. In the evening, about eight o'clock, we were drawn up in line, and our suttler, knowing that he could not get out with his goods, went down the line and gave the boys what tobacco he had on hand.

We crossed the Potomac river to the Maryland side on a pontoon bridge. Before we crossed, each Captain gave orders to his company that each man must follow his file leader and that no other orders would be given. We crossed the river by twos, the Twelfth Illinois in the front, the Eighth New York next, the Maryland and Rhode Island Cavalry in the rear, while the Colonel with his pilot went ahead with the advance to clear the road. When the head of the column got across the river, the men would start off at full speed, so by the time the last man was across, the head of the line was ten miles away.

As I belonged to Company H, I was near the rear of the line. The way we went was a caution. Each horse went as fast as he could go. By that time it was dark. Dark was no name for it! It was just the right kind of night for such an undertaking. There were roads for a short distance, which made it all the worse. The only way we could tell how far we were from our file leader was by the horses' shoes striking fire against the stones in the road. Sometimes we would be twenty yards from our file leader, and then we would come up full drive; then we would hear some tall swearing. That was the way we went for several miles. The advance drove the rebel pickets in, soon after they crossed the river. The rebels were surprised to see yankees coming from that direction. They thought we were cooped up in the Ferry and did not dare come out.

About two miles from where the rebel pickets were driven in, the rebels blockaded the road to stop us. The Colonel knew what they would do, so before he got there he went across lots and gave them the slip.

The pilot knew every foot of the ground through Maryland, and the scout knew how Longstreet's corps was situated, having come from there about an hour before we started from the Ferry. The Colonel had his route all mapped out before he started. He was bound to go through or die in the attempt. He managed to avoid the rebels until he reached Sharpsburg, where the advance had a brush with them. It was nothing but a picket force, and it was all over when the rear of the line arrived. It did not last long, as the Colonel ordered a charge and soon drove them back. The rebels retreated to camp, giving the alarm that the whole Yankee Army was upon them. We learned afterwards, by some prisoners taken at Antietam, that the whole of Longstreet's corps stood in line all the rest of the night, expecting to be attacked every minute.

As I was riding along, trying to keep up with my file leader, my horse kept shying every little while. Come to find out, there were horses lying in the road. They had been ridden so fast that they had dropped down dead by the wayside.

About two miles out, we began to go through the fields. We would go in the fields for a while, then back in the road again. At one time we were so close to the rebel camp that we could see the rebels plainly by their campfires. On we went at full speed.

I did not think at first that they were rebels. I said to my file leader—William R. Guile was my file leader—"Bill, what is the use of the Colonel going any further? Here are our troops." Bill said: "They are not our troops, they are rebels." I said to Bill, "We are goners, for we will all be captured." There was no more said then, as we had all we could attend to about that time, for we were crossing a creek, the banks of which had become so muddy, by so many horses' feet trampling them down that it was almost impossible to get through.

When the advance reached Sharpsburg, they made a halt, so we could close up and let our horses get their wind, for we had been on the keen scoot ever since we left the river. We did not stay there long, perhaps half an hour. Then on we went again, across flats, over fences, through creeks as usual. We had to travel on cross-roads, for the rebels had pickets on all main roads.

We had gone through Longstreet's corps. A great many would say that it was an impossibility for a force of about fifteen hundred cavalry to do that.

Had it not been in the night we could not have done it, and had not the Colonel managed just as he did. The rebels were taken by surprise, for they thought we had a large force. So they waited for us to attack them. But we had other business about that time. All we wanted was to get out of there. If they would let us alone, we would them.

September 15th, after some hard fighting, Harper's Ferry surrendered to Stonewall Jackson. George W. Brooks and Edward Beasley, of Company H, and several others from the regiment, were left back there on account of sickness, when we went out of the Ferry.

The first thing Stonewall said when he came into the Ferry was: "Where is that cavalry that was here yesterday?"

Some one said to him, "They left here last night."

"Which way did they go?"

"They went over into Maryland."

Stonewall Jackson said: "They can't get away. Longstreet is up in Maryland, and he has got them before this time."

After we left Sharpsburg we did not come across any more rebels until we struck the Hagerstown pike, about four miles west of Hagerstown. The pike runs east and west. Just before we got to the pike, we halted in a piece of woods. We could hear wagons rumbling along on the road ahead of us. The Colonel went ahead to reconnoitre, and when he got to the road he soon found out that it was a rebel wagon train. As soon as he saw them it came into his head to capture that train. The train was guarded by five or six hundred cavalry and a few infantry. The cavalry was in the rear of the train; the infantry was in front.

When the advance of the wagon train came along to the cross-road, the Colonel insisted that they should turn to the right, on the pike that ran to Pennsylvania. After he got the train started on that road, he sent for the Eighth New York. This was just before daylight. We went ahead and took possession of the train. The Twelfth Illinois Cavalry kept the rebel cavalry in check while we were passing by the teams to take our places.

One of the rebel teamsters said to me: "To what regiment do you belong?"

I replied: "The Eighth New York."

"The hell, you say!"

Only the drivers of a few of the head teams knew that they were prisoners; the rest did not know it until after daylight. It was a big undertaking. The Colonel might lose his whole command by doing it. At daylight we had the train on the road that ran to Green Castle. Then came the tug of war, to see if we could hold it. It was an ammunition train of seventy-five wagons, with six splendid mules hitched to each wagon. We took between two and three hundred prisoners who had crawled into the wagons to ride.

Among them was a rebel Brigadier General, an old acquaintance of Colonel Davis. The rebel had got out of the wagon and was talking with Colonel Davis. After they had talked a few minutes over old times, the rebel said to Colonel Davis:

"I suppose for old acquaintance sake, you will let me go to my command."

Colonel Davis replied: "No, sir. You will go with me."

That was enough. He went.

Luck seemed to follow us all the way through. It was one of the greatest feats of the war. After the teamsters found out that they were prisoners, weren't they mad! Mad was no name for it. They tried to stop the train. One fellow got off from his mule and began to unhitch them from the wagon. Another tried to set on fire the straw in which the shells were packed. We put a stop to that. Each man rode alongside of the driver, with revolver in hand, and we said to the rebel teamster if he "did not keep his team going, we would shoot the first man that did not obey orders." That quieted them.

So on we went. We had not gone a great many miles when we heard firing in the rear. Those of the advance thought it was all day with them then, but the rear guard kept the rebels in check. The rebel cavalry followed us up for a number of miles. The reason that the rebels did not re-take the train was that they did not know how much force we had, and were afraid to get too far north, lest they might be drawn into a trap. So they let us go with our prize.

We kept the train going as fast as we could— about ten miles an hour. We got the train through all right, and arrived in Green Castle about nine o'clock. When we arrived in Green Castle, the inhabitants at first would not believe what we had done, that we had marched from Harper's Ferry, gone through Longstreet's corps, and taken seventy-five wagons from the rebels in twelve hours.

After we had turned over the train and prisoners to the authorities of the place, we went into a piece of woods to feed our horses and rest up. We were about played out. We were hungry and sleepy, and several laid down on the ground, while others sat down with their backs leaned against a tree. Many were asleep in a jiffy.

We had not been there more than an hour when the alarm was given that the rebels were coming. The bugle sounded to horse. For all we had been up all night, we were out in line in less than five minutes. We stood there in line for a while, and as no rebels came, we went back again. Some claimed it was a false alarm, to see how quick we could get out in line. I never learned whether there was any truth in it or not.

The people in that vicinity were scared when they saw us coming; they thought we were rebels. After finding out who we were and where we had come from, and what we had done, and what a long ride we had taken, they were not long in getting there with wagons loaded with provisions for us to eat—almost everything anyone could think of—and told us to help ourselves, and we had a good square meal and some left over for another time. The boys thought that soldiering wasn't so bad after all.

From that time on, the Colonel put a great deal of confidence in the Eighth New York Cavalry. He knew that where he went, they would follow him. The boys would follow him, for they thought the Colonel could go anywhere and take them through all right. As soon as we got out of camp the boys began to like him. We soon found out that Colonel Davis was a great fighting man. To make a good regiment there must be discipline.

The regiment stayed there until the next day, when we started south again. It was in the afternoon when we arrived at the battle of Antietam. On the 17th we were not engaged, but rallied some green troops that had become demoralized and fallen back. The Eighth was on the right flank of the army and ready for any emergency. As we sat there on our horses, we could see our artillerymen work their guns. There were three batteries in a row. The men were stripped to the waist and were working their guns as fast as they could load and fire. The rebels made a charge on them, but they never got there. The enemy was driven back with great slaughter.

It has since been stated upon good authority, that the escape of the cavalry from Harper's Ferry and the capture of the wagon train, above referred to, induced the War Department to order General McClellan to make an immediate attack on Lee's army, which resulted in the memorable battle of Antietam. The capture of the wagon train was the turning point of the battle of Antietam in favor of the Union Army, because it deprived the rebels of a large amount of ammunition.

After the battle the Confederate forces began to retreat. We were ordered forward. We had quite a lively time picking up stragglers; when we came in sight of them the Captain would say:

"Corporal, take five men and go off to the right and take those five rebels over there prisoners."

Away we would go after them, and come down on them in full force. On reaching them, we would sing out:

"Surrender, Johnnies."

And they would throw down their guns and throw up their hands and yell out:

"Don't shoot, I surrender."

A great many rebels were captured in squads, anywhere from two to ten. They were almost everywhere—in barns, behind fences and in the woods. A great many stayed back on purpose to be taken prisoners. We would charge them by squads and by companies, and kept following them up.

When we arrived at the river the rebels were on the other side. They and our artillery were having a duel across the river. We came to a halt a few rods in the rear of our artillery. The right of the regiment came to a board fence. The rebel shot and shell came uncomfortably close. One shot went through the board fence, lengthwise, and made the splinters fly in all directions. We wanted to get out of there.

After about an hour, the firing stopped, and we were ordered across the river. The river, at the ford, is in a hollow, a hill on both sides; the largest hill on the south side. The Colonel marched the regiment across the river and up the hill on the other side. About two-thirds the way up, the order was countermanded and we about-faced and marched back again. It was a good thing for us that we did, for there were ten thousand rebels ambushed in the woods waiting for us. If we had gone thirty rods farther, the regiment would have been swept out of existence. There would not have been a man left to tell the tale.

After we re-crossed the river, they sent a brigade of infantry across the river. They were badly cut up and driven back. Our regiment remained there that day. Some of the boys went in to see the wounded rebels. They were in barns and houses, and in any building they could get. The rebels left all of their wounded, that could not be moved, in our hands. It was a fearful sight, every building being full for six miles around.

After the battle, the army went into camp to rest up. The Eighth New York went near Hagerstown to camp. While we were there we had about one hundred recruits come to us, and we drew some horses. They were Pennsylvania horses, and were too large for our use, and had to be turned over to the artillery.

While we were at Hagerstown, Rebel General Stuart made raids in the rear of our army with his cavalry, to capture trains and get all the horses and cattle he could. We were called upon to go for him and his troops. We followed them around without success.

One day, after we had been trying to head them off, we stopped for the night. Pickets were put out on the pike, somewhere in Maryland. There were three of us on one post. We were posted at a farm house. The barn sat close to the road, opposite the house, which stood a few rods back. Two old maids lived there. When daylight came, and they found out who we were, they prepared breakfast and gave us a polite invitation to come and eat. We went in, one at a time, and had a good breakfast. The boys were always glad to get into Maryland, for we could get something good to eat.

We kept going for them, but could not head them off. The rebels were so well posted that they escaped us every time.

In October, '62, the army commenced to move again. The cry was, "On to Richmond." The Eighth New York Cavalry moved from Hagerstown, October 25th, for Pleasant Valley. The regiment crossed the Potomac river, at Berlin, the 26th, and marched a number of miles into Virginia, and camped for the night. It was rainy, cold and a disagreeable time.

On the morning of the 27th, we broke camp and started for the rebels. We soon came upon the rebel pickets. Our cavalry was on the advance of the army. The rebel cavalry covered the retreat of their army. All the fighting that was done was cavalry against cavalry. As soon as the Union Army commenced to advance, the Confederate Army fell back to Fredericksburg, Va. As soon as we came up the rebels fell back.

We marched along until we came to Snicker's Gap, which is a road across the Blue Ridge mountains. The Colonel marched the regiment up the mountain road, to see what was there. We were marching by fours, and had gone but about one-half mile, when we found the "rebs." They had a cannon planted in the road, and when we were near enough, they fired the gun off. It was loaded with canister. The balls hit some of the horses, and made quite a commotion among the boys for a few minutes. The order was given to about-face and retreat. Away the regiment went down the road faster than they came up. The regiment did not go up there again, but marched along the foot of the mountain. This was the 27th of October.

The Eighth New York Cavalry was not brigaded until October, '62. After the battle of Antietam, and before the army moved to Fredericksburg, we were brigaded. The brigade consisted of the following regiments:

Eighth New York Cavalry, Eighth Illinois Cavalry, and three squadrons of the Third Indiana Cavalry.

Two squadrons of the Twelfth Illinois Cavalry were attached to the brigade in the spring of '63. We were the First Brigade, First Division, Cavalry Corps, Army of the Potomac.

Taking the cavalry out of Harper's Ferry put a

feather in Colonel Davis' cap. He was promoted to Brigade General. We shall have to call him General after this, but he was called Colonel more than General. He was always with the Eighth New York Cavalry. He could take the Eighth New York and make a bold and sudden dash on the rebels and accomplish more than some Generals would with a brigade.

On the first of November, we came to a place called Philamont. There we struck the rebels in force. They had found a good place and made a stand to hold us in check. When General Davis came upon the rebels, he never waited for them to attack him. He would go for them heavy. He would drive them every time he attacked them. The rebels had not got acquainted with the Eighth New York Cavalry, but it was not long before they found out who they were. The regiment made a charge on the rebels and drove them back with a big loss in killed, wounded and prisoners. We had only a few wounded.

The rebels were cautious after that how they came in contact with our sabers. After that we could not get them to stand in a charge, if they had four to our one. They knew the Eighth New York Cavalry as far as they could see them.

I do not wish to insinuate that the rebels could not fight. There were just as brave men on one side as the other, but the men on the Union side were fighting for the right, which made them braver. They were fighting for the Stars and Stripes, the emblem of liberty, the flag that our forefathers fought under. The rebels could not stand in front of the Union Army in an open field fight. We drove the rebels back to Union, where they made a stand.

November 2d, as Company H was standing in line, waiting for orders, General Davis ordered Captain Barry to take his company and charge on some rebel skirmishers. About forty rods from there was a hollow. The rebels would walk up the slope so that they could look over, fire at us and then fall back out of sight, before we could fire at them. The rebels in the hollow were in a southwest direction from us. Instead of going that way we charged west from where we were. After we had gone about one hundred and sixty rods, we came up in front of a piece of woods. There were rebel skirmishers in the woods.

About the time we halted, the rebels fired at us and wounded David Shippey, Jr. It was at first supposed to be fatal; but by good health, strong constitution and good care, he got through and is living to-day. The ball went through his right lung, coming out close to the backbone. No one else was hit.

After David Shippey was taken to the rear, the company turned south and marched along the edge of the woods until we got past it. We then came in full view of a rebel battery, off at our right. When we came in sight, the rebels turned one gun on us and commenced to fire. We marched along for about twenty rods, then we took a left turn and circled around back where we started from.

While we were marching back, the "rebs" were firing away at us all the time. A six pound solid shot struck and went through the shoulder blades of the horse that Nicholas Wiler was riding but, did not hurt Nicholas. He was number "one" in the four. The other three horses were a little lower and out of line, which saved them. The horse never stopped, but kept right along with the rest for fifty rods, when he halted. After he stopped, he could not move again. Walter B. Norton was left back to take care of David Shippey. He shot the horse and put him out of his misery. The rebels soon fell back.

November 3d, we came upon the rebels again' near Upperville. We halted in a piece of woods. Company H was ordered to dismount and fight on foot. Every fourth man stayed with the horses, while the rest went to fight on foot. We marched along until we came to the edge of the woods. At the edge of the woods was a stone wall. When we came to the wall, one of the men saw a "reb" off about half a mile, and fired at him without orders. There was a rebel battery off at our right, and when they heard the shot, they turned their guns that way and commenced firing. We must have been just the right distance off, for the shells exploded right over our heads, the pieces flying around so that we were ordered to lie down by the wall.

I lay hugging the wall as close as I could, while

Sergeant Cheney lay stretched out a few feet from the wall. He said to me:

"What makes you hug the wall so?"

About that time a shell exploded and a piece came down and struck so close to his leg that he got up to that wall in a hurry.

He did not say any more.

Soon we heard a yell. It was General Davis with the rest of the regiment, charging the rebels. We went back to where our horses were, mounted, and on we went.

The General, when he came up where the rebels were, would cast his eyes over the field, and he could tell in a minute what to do. He would take them on the flank and would go for them heavy, and rout them in a hurry.

So on we went towards Fredericksburg. We got the rebels flying, and drove them through Upperville, across the plain into the mountains. The rebels got their battery into position and threw a few shells at us without any damage to us.

Leaving them, we marched back through Upperville. About half a mile from there, the regiment camped for the night. Our provisions were out, our wagons having failed to get there. There was plenty of forage for our horses, but not for us. The boys used to go in the cornfields, take a shock of corn and give it to their horses. They would soon make a cornfield look small.

That night something had to be done. We had had nothing to eat that day. Davis was a man who wanted his men and horses to have enough to eat. Horses were looked after, first. There were strict orders that no man should molest anything that belonged to the inhabitants through the country.

General Davis soon had four or five men detailed to go out and get some cattle. They had not been gone long before they came back with two fat cattle for beef. They soon had them dressed and dealt out to the men. We ate that beef clear, nothing with it. Some ate it without any salt. William R. Guile and I were tent mates. We kept salt with us all the time, and gave some to those that did not have any.

The next morning, we started again. The rebels did not make a stand again until the 5th, at Barber's Cross Roads. On the morning of the 5th, we commenced our march again. General Pleasanton was with the brigade that day. We marched along until the middle of the afternoon, when we came to Barber's Cross Roads. The rebels had made a stand to hold us in check. When we came within a mile of Barber's Cross Roads, we went into the fields. The Eighth New York Cavalry went to the right, while the rest of the brigade took the left of the road.

After marching nearly one hundred rods, we came to a knoll that hid us from view. There we halted, and the General dismounted Company I and one other company to fight on foot.

The General was quite a smoker. He had an old clay, pipe and when he got engaged he would keep his pipe in his mouth for an hour after it was smoked out. The boys knew that there was going to be business that day, for he had his pipe in his mouth bottom side up. There was a stone wall that ran from where we were to within about twenty yards from the rebel battery. The General was bound to take that battery, but he did not quite do it. The dismounted soldiers could, by stooping over, work themselves along the wall and not be seen by the rebels. They were to go such a distance and draw the attention of the rebels, while the General would charge the battery with the rest of the regiment.

After the men on foot had gone on, the General marched the mounted portion of the regiment by twos, over the knoll, straight at the rebel battery. The knoll was about sixty rods from the battery. When the head of the line had arrived about half way to the battery, the General halted us and went off to see how the land lay, as the boys used to call it.

As soon as we came in sight, the rebels commenced to fire at us; but we were so close that the shells went over and beyond us before they exploded. Then we had to stand and let them shoot at us. The shells went straight over our heads. We expected every minute that a shot would rake the whole line; but for some reason, we could not tell what, the rebels could not get their guns to bear low enough. There was nothing in the way as we could see. So there we sat on our horses, expecting the next shot would rake down through us. Standing as we were, in a straight line, if a shot had got low enough, it would have been fearful. It would have gone through the whole line and would have killed and wounded about every one.

The boys were so close to them that they could see the rebels work their guns plainly. We would watch the man when he pulled the layzard, and when he gave the string a yank, we would duck our heads and hug our horses' necks as close as possible. I know that I made myself as small as I could.

It was rough to keep us there to be shot at in that way. If the General had given orders to charge the battery, we would have liked it better then; in fact, all that saved us was being so close to the battery. The man on the left of me would sit up straight as a bean pole on his horse when a shot would come over. He said to me:

"What makes you bend over so, you will get hit just the same."

I replied to him.

"I can't help it; those shells are coming pretty close."

It seemed that the shells did not go over two feet from our heads. We were there about fifteen minutes, although it seemed a great deal longer than that.

At the time, I could not imagine what General Davis kept us there in that way for. I found out before the war closed. To make veteran soldiers the Generals must have their men under fire. The troops that could stand such a fire as that, would go any where.

Off to the right of us was a regiment of rebel cavalry in line, watching the firing. They must have laughed a little when they saw us ducking our heads. Those who laugh last, laugh best. We were glad when Davis came and marched us down under the knoll, out of range. The General found more rebels there than he expected to. The Eighth New York Cavalry were the only troops there, the rest of the brigade being on the other side of the road, and had the battery with them. The Eighth New York was fighting three regiments of rebels and a battery of four guns.

After we went under the knoll, out of range, the rebels lost track of us. They had found out where the dismounted horses were, and made a charge on them. Then the General got in one of his counter charges. The General had been watching the rebels. We could not see them, but heard them yell.

It was not long before the General came over the knoll and gave the command to right wheel and come on. We went up over that knoll kiting, and came together heavy. It was cut and slash. When the rebels saw us, they were under such headway that a good many of them could not stop their horses, and rode past us and were taken prisoners. Those who could, wheeled their horses and got out. We went for them heavy, and killed a number and wounded a good many. It will never be known how many were wounded. A large number of them clung to their horses' necks and were taken back to the rear. We took about fifty prisoners.

While we were all mixed up together, the rebel artillery kept throwing shells in among us; but all the execution they did was to their own men. Orderly Sergeant Hopkins, of Company H, got after a rebel Major. He did not quite get him. He got close enough to give him a saber wound across the shoulder. The rebel escaped.

There were only three or four of our men wounded. The dismounted soldiers behind the wall, got in a cross fire on the rebels, and gave them "Hail Columbia." The other two regiments of rebels were in line about forty rods away. I guess that they were afraid of us, or else they thought we had more troops there somewhere. The rebels had about twenty-five hundred men in their three regiments, while we had five hundred and fifty in our regiment. All that saved the Eighth New York was the General's counter-charge. If he had waited until the rebels had proceeded any farther, it would have been all day with the Eighth New York Cavalry.

Off on the hill, about a mile from there, General Pleasanton was watching the Eighth New York. When the rebels made the charge on us, the General said to one of his aides:

"The Eighth New York is a goner."

When he saw that we had driven the rebels back, he slapped his hands and yelled out:

"Bully for the Eighth New York!"

When he first saw what shape we were in, he ordered the Third Indiana Cavalry to support us.

They arrived just as we had finished with that regiment of rebels, so the rebels dusted out of that in a hurry. Soon our battery came and gave the rebels a few parting shots. Then we went in camp for the night.

The next day we started again, arriving at Amosville on the 7th of November. We drove the rebels out of there and kept going on. We arrived at Jefferson, November 13th. Here we had followed the rebels until they were so well reinforced that further fighting against greater odds would only amount to a failure. The weather had commenced to grow cold and the men had no shelter tents. We suffered from the weather.

We camped at Jefferson over night. The rebels had been through there, and stripped everything in the place except some hives of honey. We were not allowed to molest anything that belonged to the inhabitants, but that night the boys were let loose. I suppose the officers thought that we could not get anything, so they let us go in. We took the hives and carried them out in the lot and took the honey out, ate some and destroyed the rest. I know that the next day William Guile and I had some cooked chicken in our haversack.

We started the next day, took a cross road and went over on the road where the main army was marching. A short distance from there, we had to go down a hill into a valley. When we had nearly reached the foot of the hill, we heard a yell off at our left, and looking in that direction saw a regiment of rebel cavalry charging down on us. We were marching by fours. I thought that the Colonel would form us in line to receive them, but he paid no attention to them. The rebels came near enough to see what regiment it was, then halted and went back.

As we crossed the creek, the rear of our wagon train was passing. Back upon the hill about half a mile, the rebels got a battery in position and commenced to throw shells into our wagons. Almost the first shot hit the rear end of one of the wagons. It did not do much damage, but scared the driver so that he left his team and was going to dig out. But he was driven back to his team, and on they went.

Soon one of our batteries of light artillery got into position and commenced to fire on the rebels. The rebels being so much higher, our battery could not get their shots up there. The rebels got a good range on our battery, and they put the shells right down there every time. All the rest of the troops had gone on. They sent on and had a twenty pound battery come back. They got their guns into position and commenced firing. They put the shells right in among the rebels. They did not wait for any more, but skedaddled back into the woods. That was the last we saw of them.

We had a brush with the rebels at Sulphur Springs, November 15th. Then we marched with the main army to Fredericksburg, arriving there about the 24th. Then we were sent to guard Banks' Ford, on the Rappahannock river.

After we had been there a few days, one of the rebels on the other side of the river yelled out to me:

"Hello, Yank!"

He received no answer at first, and he yelled out again:

"Yank, come over here."

I replied that if he wished to see me he must come where I was. It was not long before he started to come over. When he was about half way across, I asked him what he wanted, and told him he could not play any game on me. He replied:

"It is all right between you and me. I don't want to harm you. I want to trade with you. Do you want to trade horses?"

I said: "No."

He replied: "All right; but I would like to trade some tobacco for some coffee."

I told him I would be glad to trade with him. I saw that he meant no harm to me, so I told him to come up on the bank where I was. When he arrived, the first thing he asked was:

"What regiment do you belong to?"

I told him the Eighth New York Cavalry. He said:

"I belong to the Second North Carolina Cavalry. Do you remember the cavalry fight at Barber's Cross Roads?"

I told him I thought I did.

Said he:

"That was my regiment that you fellows charged.

The Eighth New York Cavalry is the worst regiment we ever had any fighting with. They can handle the saber to perfection. You fellows gave our regiment gowdy."

We talked a while and then we traded. I gave him some coffee for a quantity of tobacco, and he re-crossed the river. The rebel pickets used to trade quite often with our boys, but we were obliged to be shy and not let our officers know it, for it was strictly against orders.

We had not been there long before we got out of forage for our horses, and had to go back in the country and get hay. Instead of drawing it in wagons, we used to bring it on horseback. We would take our surcingle and halter and tie them around a bundle of hay and then put it on our horses and march to camp. The boys had lived on hard tack and salt pork so long that they wanted a change. When we went along, we used to see hogs running around in the woods, so we contrived a plan to get them. We could not shoot them, so we got two or three men on their horses to go and drive the hogs out. Then ten or fifteen of us with our sabers would scatter along on foot, and when the hogs came along we would hit them a whack over their heads, and down they would go. That was the way we got our fresh pork.

We guarded the Ford for about two weeks, when we were sent ten miles below Fredericksburg to guard a ferry and do picket duty in King George county. While were doing duty there, the boys used to go to the quarters of the colored people in that vicinity to get them to make us hoe cake for a change. A hoe cake is made out of the same materials as water johnny cake, only it is fried in a spider instead of baking it.

As I was out one day to get a hoe cake, I went by a nice plantation. A young lady came to the door and gave me a polite invitation to come in. She had heard so much about the yankees that she wanted to see and talk with one. All the people on the plantation were two young ladies, their mother and a few servants. Their father and two brothers were in the Rebel Army. We talked about the war. One of the young ladies said that in '61 a company of young men enlisted right in their neighborhood for the Rebel Army. The young ladies said that at the time the company was raised, they thought that one company could whip all the yankees. They had faith at that time that the rebels would carry the day.

We were guarding the Ferry the 13th of December, the day the great battle of Fredericksburg was fought. We could hear the roar of artillery from where we were. It was boom and crash all day long. It must have been fearful to march up to those guns and be mowed down without accomplishing anything.

CHAPTER IV.

BUILDING WINTER QUARTERS—SHORT STAY—BURNSIDE'S STRATEGY—BUILDING FIRES—BURNSIDE STUCK IN THE MUD—STAFFORD COURT HOUSE—PICKETING AT DUMFRIES—GUERRILLAS—BUSHWHACKERS—SNOW—COLD WEATHER.

AFTER the battle, the Union Army crossed back over the river again. We were soon relieved. We went into camp near Bell Plain Landing. It was "Hurrah, boys, build winter quarters, we are going to stay here." We went to work and built log houses, four men to a house, and built a corduroy for our horses. We had just settled down when we were ordered away. We remained just about two weeks. That was the last of our building winter quarters that winter, for we were kept going most of the time. Everything was quiet on the Potomac for the present.

About the 20th of January, '63, the army attempted to cross the river the second time; or, "Burnside stuck in the mud," as it was called. If the weather had proved favorable, Burnside would have been all right; he would have whipped the rebels out of their boots.

On the night of the 19th, just before dark, the Eighth New York had orders to get ready for a march. The night was dark and looked like rain.

The boys wondered where we were going. Some said one place, and some another; but none of them could guess right. About an hour's march brought us opposite to the Ferry, ten miles below Fredericksburg. About two miles back from the river, on the hill, we were ordered to halt and secure our horses.

Then came the order to build fires. We scattered all over that hill, and commenced to build fires to make the rebels think the army was going to cross the river at that point. It proved to be a great success, for the rebels had seen the fires, and a portion of their army was ordered down to the Ferry. After we had built fires for a while, it commenced to rain. The hills were well illuminated by this time. It rained as hard as it could pour down all the rest of the night. We were wet through in a short time. My tentmate and I came along where a tree had been blown over by the roots, and we built a fire behind that and stayed there all night.

It was Burnside's intention to draw the rebels out of their fortified position and then cross the river above Fredericksburg. The rebels had seen the fires that we had built, and they thought the yankees were down there sure enough. When daylight came, Burnside and his army were down near the river with his artillery stuck in the mud. No one knows what Virginia mud is until they have been there. The rebels saw them and yelled out and asked them if they wanted them to come over and help them out. The rebels on the other side of the river nailed a board on a post, and wrote on it: "Burnside stuck in the mud," in letters large enough to be read on this side of the river. The Union Army marched back into camp again, while the rebels marched back into their fortification on Marye's Heights. All was quiet again.

About the 1st of February, '63, the regiment went into camp near Stafford Court House. The headquarters of the regiment was kept there until April.

When we went out we had only nine companies; the other three companies were raised and sent on to us. They arrived about the first of January, '63.

On the 21st of February, three squadrons started for Dumfries to do picket duty. The place was a wilderness grown up with scrub oak and pine. It commenced to snow that night, and it snowed that night and all the next day. The snow fell to the depth of twelve inches, and it came off cold, but did not last long. As we were marching along on the 22d, we met an old Virginian. One officer asked him how far it was to such a place. He answered:

"Right smart ways."

I never found out how far that is. The boys used to have it for a by-word after that.

We had a rough time doing picket duty. It was so cold one night that Stephen Scott and several others froze their feet so that their boots had to be cut off from them. It was so cold one night when I was on picket, that I got off from my horse and walked around to keep my feet from freezing. The order was not to dismount. I thought if the rebels had as hard a time to keep warm as I did, they would not trouble us any. In about a week the weather changed; then it was mud.

Back at the reserve we had a fire. We had rails laid up to keep us out of the snow, and we would roast one side a while, and then turn around and warm the other side.

The guerillas and bushwhackers troubled us a great deal. They would steal up in the daytime and shoot men at their posts. They killed and wounded quite a number in that way. At that time the rebels knew just as much about our army as our Generals did. They even knew how many men we had in every regiment, the names of the officers and when we had any new recruits. The rebels knew that we had three new companies in our regiment. We thought it was queer how they knew it, but we found out after a time. The old men who were not able to carry arms in the rebel service were left behind. When the Union soldiers were around they would pretend to be Unionists and would find out all that was going on. Then they would go in the night and communicate with the rebels.

When any of the old companies were on picket, everything would be all right; but as soon as any of the new companies went on picket and on the same posts, the rebels would go for them, and they captured quite a number of them. The next night after the rebels attacked the new company, one of the old companies was sent out in the same place to see if they would come again. They did not come near; the rebels knew when we made the change every time.

In the night of March 5th, the rebels broke through the picket line of Company K, killed two, wounded two and captured seventeen of them. The author was wounded on picket, March 29th, by a gunshot wound in the left hand with the loss of one finger. At night we used to change the posts in different places from those we had in the daytime. Some of the old men inside of our lines would go through them in the daytime and come back in the night. By our changing posts, they would run on to the pickets when they returned.

The post that I was on that night was among scrub pine. There was a place just large enough for a horse to stand. All around was a dense growth of pine. It was about twelve o'clock at night, when one of the bushwhackers, coming back through our lines, ran onto me. I never heard or saw him until he was within twenty feet of me. He probably never saw me until then. He fired first. He could not have taken any aim, if he had he would have shot me through the body. As soon as he fired, he started and ran. I let drive at him, but probably did not hit him, as we never saw anything more of him.

Our officers used to arrest some of them and send them to Washington. All they would do at

Washington was to make them take the oath of allegiance and let them go. The "reb" would go back home and do the same thing over again.

The regiment was relieved by the Third Indiana Cavalry. Then we went back to our camp, at Stafford Court House. We remained there until the 13th of April, when we started for the Rappahannock river.

CHAPTER V.

THE CAVALRY ON THE MOVE—SKIRMISHING—FORAGING—CROSSING THE RAPIDAN—BATTLE OF CHANCELLORSVILLE—RECROSSING THE RIVER—IN CAMP—THE MARCH TO BEVERLY FORD—THE BATTLE OF BEVERLY FORD—DEATH OF GENERAL DAVIS, CAPTAIN FOOTE AND LIEUTENANT CUTLER—LEE'S INVASION—A GREAT MARCH—FIGHT AT MIDDLEBURG—CROSSING THE POTOMAC RIVER INTO MARYLAND AGAIN—THE MARCH TO GETTYSBURG—THE BATTLE OF GETTYSBURG.

WE were on the move at an early hour, April 13th, 1863, and marched to some place between Elk Run and Morgansburg, and camped for the night at about eight o'clock. The whole brigade was on the move, with prospects that we were going to cross the Rappahannock soon. Out the next morning and on the road to Morgansburg; from there moved toward Warrenton. But before arriving at the latter place, we bore to the left and went into camp about noon.

The next day we started for Freeman's Ford, on the Rappahannock. We crossed the Ford and went about three miles, when the regiment came upon the rebel pickets at a ford upon Hagle Run. The regiment charged them across the Ford, and took about twelve prisoners; after which the regiment moved down the run below the forks, where the regiment re-crossed the Rappahannock at Beverly Ford. The enemy charged upon our rear guard, and captured three of them. The rebels fired across the Ford upon the fourth squadron, which was guarding it, and wounded Lieutenant Webster, of Company I. They then skedaddled out of sight. They threw a few shells, but they did no damage.

We encamped there for the night, and next day went out foraging. About three miles from camp, we found some corn and confiscated it, with a quantity of beef, tobacco and other articles. We broke camp the next day, and marched to Liberty, where we halted, but were soon ordered on again, and marched to near Warrenton, where the regiment camped for the night. The next day the regiment started, about 10 o'clock A. M., and marched into Warrenton, made a left-about and marched back to our camp at Liberty. We stayed there that night.

The next day the regiment packed up and started about noon, and marched in the direction of Warrenton, till within about three miles of it, when the regiment turned to the left and marched about six miles and camped for the night. It was muddy travelling. The regiment stayed there the next day, and then moved up through Warrenton and camped near the railroad.

The regiment remained there and did picket duty and some foraging until April 28th, there being rain and mud as usual, when they moved to Rappahannock Station, where we arrived about 4 o'clock A. M. April 29th. We fed our horses and were on the move again at half past seven and marched to Kelley's Ford, halted a couple of hours, after which we forded the river and formed in line of battle, and started in the direction of Culpepper. We went about three miles and camped, after driving the rebels out of that place. It was raining.

April 30th—The boys were up at sunrise and groomed and fed their horses, after which the regiment was ordered into line, and about 7 o'clock commenced moving again in the direction of Culpepper, at which place the regiment arrived in the neighborhood of 11 A. M., and passed through without any opposition, and made a halt of two hours; then took up our line of march for the Rapidan, where the regiment arrived about sundown. The rebels threw two or three shells at us, which brought the regiment to a halt. After driving the enemy back, we went into camp in the woods. Rain, and muddy travelling.

May 1st—A part of the regiment went foraging, but was not successful, the rebels being a little too close with their artillery to make it very pleasant, to say nothing about it being dangerous. The day was spent in skirmishing and artillery firing, with no great advantage on either side.

May 2d—We got up and saddled, and moved out of camp to support a battery, but there was no firing, and at 9 o'clock A. M. we took our line of march in the direction of Culpepper, but passed to the right of it and halted at Stevensburg, and allowed our horses to graze a couple of hours, after which we moved again toward the Rapidan, where we arrived about midnight, and were going into camp, but the rebels fired upon one of the camps, and it was thought best to move a little farther from the river. Nearly one-half of the regiment dismounted and went down and guarded the Ford; the rest went into camp.

May 3d—We were up in the morning and took care of our horses, and about 9 o'clock A. M. moved across the Rapidan. About noon we were within the lines of General Hooker's army, and shortly were at United States Ford. The regiment was not very extensively engaged at the battle of Chancellorsville. They were on the left flank of our army. But the regiment suffered from the weather. It rained most of the time. From the noise of the cannon and musket firing, there was a heavy battle fought on the 3d of May. The regiment re-crossed the river the 4th of May.

May 5th—Up at 3 o'clock A. M. and on the road to Falmouth, where the regiment arrived about 7 o'clock A. M., and halted about three hours; then moved again up the river and passed Hanwood Church and experienced one of the hardest showers that was ever known.

May 6th—Moved camp near to the Widow Kemper's Ford, and the boys were sent to work on fortifications. Worked the next day.

May 8th—Were on picket at the Ford. Called up that night and joined the brigade.

May 9th—We were up all night, marching and standing to horse. Moved to Potomac Creek and went into camp. From that time, there was not much going on, only picket duty and dress parade, inspection, washing clothes, etc., until June 6th. The regiment moved camp once to Brooks' Station within that time.

June 6th—We were all ready for a move, forage and rations on hand, and at two o'clock " Boots and saddles " was sounded, and five o'clock found us on the move.

June 7th—On the march nearly all night from Brooks' Station to Stafford Court House, and from Stafford in the direction of Hanwood. But the advance losing their way, we twisted and doubled around, and did not arrive at the place until three in the morning, when the regiment fed and slept for about two hours. The boys were called up again, fed their horses, groomed them, and made a cup of coffee, then mounted and marched for Warrenton Junction, where the regiment arrived about two o'clock, made a short halt, and then moved to Catlitt's Station, where they went into camp for the night.

June 28th—We did not start until 5 o'clock P. M., and then moved in the direction of Beverton's Station. From Beverton Station the regiment marched to Beverly Ford, and arrived there about midnight; laid down and slept for a while. On the morning of the 9th of June, the boys were up early, fed their horses and saddled up, and at daylight started for the Ford. The regiment was on the advance across the river. There was a heavy fog over the river, so it was impossible to see but a short distance. When the advance of the regiment reached the other side of the river, they came in close contact with the rebel picket before he saw them. He was ordered to surrender before he could give the alarm. A few rods from the river was stationed the picket reserve. General Davis ordered Company B to charge on them. The first volley fired took effect on Lieutenant Cutler, the ball striking him in the neck and killing him almost instantly. At that time there was a great commotion in the rebel camp. Along the river bank, for a few rods back, was timber; back of that was cleared land in places. The rebels were there and had their horses out grazing. Some were up and partly dressed, some were cooking breakfast when the first firing was heard. The rebels had to cook their own food. They had flour or meal dealt out to them and had to cook it the best way they could. They had no hard tack. The rebel officers were yelling "To horse!" and the rebels were running in all directions. The Eighth New York charged through the woods. By that time the rebels charged on the regiment with a large force, and, firing at the same time, killed General Davis and Captain Foote, of Company E. The last words Davis said were : "Stand firm, Eighth New York!" The rebels were only a few rods off when they shot General Davis. The regiment fell back under cover of the woods and waited for reinforcements.

General Davis was in the regular service, and before the war was posted in one of the Southern States. Some of the rebels knew him. They were bound to kill him because he would not fight on their side.

We were soon reinforced by the Eighth Illinois and Third Indiana Cavalry and went in again. We drove the rebels back for a ways, and took some prisoners. Then the rebels were reinforced, and drove us back in turn and took some prisoners from us. We were reinforced and sailed in again. Finally, the rebels were driven back to stay.

Riley Lowe, of Company H, was wounded and taken prisoner in the early part of the day. The rebels had taken his horse and equipments from him and told him to march along with them on foot, but about that time our cavalry made a charge on them. They dug out and left their prisoners. To keep from being run over, Lowe laid down by the side of a log. He said the horses from both sides passed over him a number of times.

The Eighth New York fought for all they were worth. They were bound to avenge the General's death. The rebels were going to have a review of their cavalry on that day, but our boys reviewed them. It was a big cavalry fight. All that saved Rebel General Stuart's cavalry was their being reinforced with infantry. From that day the rebel cavalry could not stand in front of our cavalry for an hour.

That day General Davis was acting General of the Division. Had he lived through that battle, he would have been made Division General. William D. Adams was killed, and Riley Lowe and Charley

Geer, of Company H, were wounded. There were eight killed and fifteen wounded in the regiment.

Our cavalry fell back across the river that night. It was a mystery to the boys why they fell back. The head officers knew all about it. That day the private papers of General Stuart were captured. They told Lee's plans. He was already on the move north with his main army. Then came one of the greatest marches ever known. The Army of the Potomac had to make quick time to keep Lee from Washington and Baltimore. The cavalry marched on the flank of Lee's army.

June 10*th*—The regiment moved from Beverly Ford to Catlitt's Station and went into camp, remaining there until June 15th, when it moved through Manassas Junction to Bull Run.

June 17*th*—Started about noon and marched to Aldie. One squadron were on picket that night.

June 18*th*—The regiment moved in the direction of Snicker's Gap, skirmishing with the rebels and driving them beyond Belmont, then returned to Aldie and bivouacked for the night.

June 21*st*—At daylight were on the move in the direction of Middleburg, passed through the place and about two miles beyond, where the regiment found the rebels, attacked them and drove them beyond Upperville, where we bivouacked for the night.

June 22*d*—Moved back near Aldie, where the regiment went out to find the rebels, but without success. Stayed in that vicinity until June 26th, when the regiment marched to Leesburg.

June 27th—Moved from Leesburg to Edwards' Ferry, crossed the Potomac river and marched to near Point of Rocks and bivouacked.

June 28th—Up at daylight and marched to Middletown and remained over night.

June 29th—Started at 9 o'clock A. M., marched through South Mountain, Boonsboro and crossed the mountain in the direction of Gettysburg.

June 30th—Up at 2 A. M. and at daylight resumed our march toward Fairfield, but finding a force of rebels in that town and not wishing to bring on an engagement at that point, counter-marched through Emmetsburg, and from there to Gettysburg, making the rebels leave in a hurry. One squadron was on picket that night.

July 1st—Came the great battle of Gettysburg. The first division of cavalry, commanded by General Buford, was the first to get there. The first division of cavalry and the first corps of infantry were the troops that saved the battle of Gettysburg. The cavalry kept the rebels in check for two hours, so the first corps could get into position. The first corps kept the rebels in check for four hours. By that time reinforcements came. At 2 o'clock, the Union troops fell back to Cemetery Hill. If the rebels had got in possession of Cemetery Hill, Round Top and Little Round Top the first day, history would be different than it is now. The Eighth New

York Cavalry lost brave Captain Follett, of Company D, and one man from Company M, killed in a charge in which the rebels were severely repulsed and a large number of them taken prisoners. The regiment was on picket again that night.

July 2d—The regiment formed in line of battle upon the left, supporting the sharpshooters. It left the field at 11 o'clock and the division moved to Taneytown. The Eighth New York was highly praised by the Generals for what it did on the first day.

July 3d—Moved from Taneytown to near Westminster and went into camp. Heavy fighting at Gettysburg yet. Our horses about starved.

CHAPTER VI.

THE REBELS RETREAT—THE CAVALRY ON THE MOVE—SKIRMISHING—FIGHT AT FUNKSTOWN—CAPTURE OF A REBEL GUN—ACROSS THE POTOMAC RIVER INTO VIRGINIA AGAIN—TRAVELLING THE SAME GROUND OVER AGAIN—RAPPAHANNOCK STATION—ON PICKET—GERMANIA FORD—MADISON COURT HOUSE—BRANDY STATION—CULPEPPER—KELLY'S FORD—DRIVING THE REBELS SOUTH OF RAPIDAN—WINTER QUARTERS—THE EIGHTH NEW YORK CAVALRY'S TRANSFER TO THE SECOND BRIGADE, THIRD DIVISION, APRIL, '64—CROSSING THE RAPIDAN—THE RAID TO RICHMOND, MAY, '64—GRANT'S FLANK MOVEMENT—WHITE HOUSE LANDING—MALVERN HILL—JAMES RIVER—PETERSBURG—THE WILSON RAID IN JUNE, '64.

THE regiment moved, July 4th, 1863, from camp, four miles in the direction of Frederick, and bivouacked for the night. A very rainy time.

July 5th—Up early in the morning and moved to Frederick, where we drew rations, moved through the town and bivouacked for the night.

July 6th—The regiment was ordered to pack everything for a long march, and that day moved on through Middletown, South Mountain and Boonsboro, to near Williamsport, where we found a force of rebels, which we engaged until dark, and then returned to Jones' Cross Roads and bivouacked. The regiment had a number wounded.

July 7th—Moved from Jones' Cross Roads back to Boonsboro and camped.

July 8th—Rainy again. About 11 o'clock we were attacked by the rebels and fought with them all day. We succeeded in driving them from the field. The regiment had several wounded.

July 9th—Out again. Found the rebels about 5 p. m. and made them get up and get. Sergeant Miner was wounded.

July 10th—At the rebels again and drove them to Funkstown, where they stopped us and undertook to drive us back, but they did not succeed. The infantry came up and relieved us, and the regiment fell back and camped. We lost two killed and several wounded.

July 11th—Moved to Barbersville and did picket duty until the 14th.

July 14th—Up at an early hour, Company H squadron deployed as skirmishers and moved about three miles before they found the rebels. Company H squadron captured one gun, took a large number of prisoners and returned to our last night's camp.

July 15th—Moved through Sharpsburg, Sandy Hook and Knoxville, to Berlin. The next day moved camp to Fetersville.

July 18th—About 2 p. m. crossed the Potomac and were in Virginia again. Camped near Sevettsville that night.

July 19th—Up and on the move. Marched within four miles of Upperville, bivouacked for the night.

July 20th—Moved to left of Upperville and made a stop of two hours at Wrecktentown, then marched about eight miles and bivouacked.

July 21st—Our regiment on the advance. Moved

around to the left of Barber's Cross Roads and up into Chester's Gap, where we found a nest of rebels. Fell back about two miles and camped. John Reynolds and one of the men of Company M were wounded.

The next day the rebels attacked us and drove us back to Barber's Cross Roads. Plenty to eat for men and horses, but the pickets are getting out of tobacco.

July 24th—Drew rations.

July 25th—The first squadron went out scouting in search of horses, obtained quite a number and found some corn. Returned to camp at dark.

July 26th—Marched from Barber's Cross Roads to Liberty.

July 27th—Moved to near Rappahannock Station and went into camp. Stayed there until August 1st.

August 1st—Up at 1 o'clock A. M., packed and saddled at 3 A. M. Moved down to the ford and waited until the pontoon bridge was laid, after which the regiment moved up the railroad about two miles and found the rebels. Engaged them and drove them to within two or three miles of Culpepper, and finding the rebels in force, fell back to within about two miles of Rappahannock Station. One squadron on picket.

August 3d—Kept the horses saddled all day in anticipation of an attack.

August 4th—Were attacked by the rebels, but drove them beyond the picket line. The regiment was on picket from that time until the 9th.

EIGHTH NEW YORK CAVALRY. 73

August 9th—Moved camp across the river and below the Station, not far from Kelly's Ford.

August 11th—On picket all day and night again.

August 15th—Marched to Catlitt's Station, then in a northeast direction about five miles and camped. The regiment did picket duty, foraging, etc., until August 31st.

August 31st—Moved to Harwood, from there to Falmouth.

September 2d—Remained in camp until 5 P. M., when Company H squadron moved out upon picket, headquarters of the squadron at the Lacy House, opposite Fredericksburg. Remained on picket until the 3d, when they joined the regiment at Harwood.

September 4th—Took an early start and arrived at Catlitt's Station about noon and went into camp.

September 13th—Crossed the Rappahannock river and drove the rebels about four miles beyond Culpepper, where we camped for the night. Gimmet and Sergeant Kazoo, of Company M, were wounded.

September 14th—Marched to Raccoon Ford, on the Rapidan, where we found the rebels again. The sharpshooters on both sides tried their skill across the river. There was also some artillery practice. They kept that up for two or three days. Nicholas Wiler, of Company H, was wounded and lost his arm.

September 19th—Company H and G squadron were ordered out scouting. They went to Germania Ford on the Rapidan, where some of the boys charge across and took four prisoners, and returned to camp about sundown.

September 21st—On the move at 7 A. M. Passed Culpepper and proceeded to near Madison Court House and bivouacked for the night.

September 22d—Marched through Madison Court House towards the Rapidan. About 11 A. M., found the rebels, engaged them and drove them back. After the fight, moved down the river about eight miles and camped for the night. The next day, marched back to the old camp at Stevensburg, where we arrived about sundown.

September 25th—Up at an early hour, moved to within about half a mile of Germania Ford and sent out pickets. On picket the next day.

September 29th—Moved from Germania Ford to within a short distance of the junction of the two rivers and went upon picket again. Stayed there until October 10th.

October 10th—Broke camp and moved to Germania Ford, charged across and took about twenty prisoners. Moved from there to Morton's Ford and bivouacked.

October 11th—Commenced fighting about 8 A. M., and were at it all day, the rebels driving the regiment back to Rappahannock Station. Billy Patterson was killed; Daniel Nellis, Daniel Kehoe, wounded, and Daniel Campbell missing. Enos Guile's horse was wounded. The cavalry drove the rebels beyond Brandy Station. In the afternoon Captain Barry was wounded.

October 13th—From Rappahannock to Warrenton Junction.

October 14th—From the Junction to Brentsville, the rebels following close with the intention of capturing the wagon train. Hard fighting that day. Left Brentsville that night about 7 o'clock, were in the saddle all night and arrived at Fairfax Station about 7 o'clock, on the morning of the 15th. The regiment did picket duty in that vicinity until November 8th, the division crossed the Rappahannock, through Jeffersonville, crossed Hagle Run and moved in the direction of Culpepper, and had a fight in the afternoon. Moved to the left of Culpepper to Brandy Station, from there to Rappahannock Station and camped. From that camp to Culpepper again.

The regiment did picket duty until November 26th, when it left the camp near Culpepper and moved through Stevensburg. A part of the regiment was sent off towards Kelly's Ford and went into camp about 8 o'clock. Heard cannonading on our right.

November 27th—Moved from our last night's camp to Ellis Ford and sent out our pickets. Heavy firing in the direction of Germania Ford that day. Were relieved and joined the brigade near Richardsville.

In the fall of '63, the ground between the Rappahannock and Rapidan rivers was fought over two or three times. The rebels wanted to keep the Union Army north of the Rappahannock; but in November the Union Army succeeded in driving the rebels back across the Rapidan river and they stayed there the rest of the winter of '63 and '64. From December, '63 until April '64, the regiment was doing picket duty, scouting, etc. In April, '64 the Eighth New York Cavalry was transferred to the Second Brigade, Third Division, General Wilson commanding. The brigade consisted of the following regiments: Eighth New York, Twenty-Second New York, First Vermont and First New Hampshire Cavalry.

May 4th, '64—Called up at 3 o'clock in the morning, and started from our camp at 6 o'clock and marched to Germania Ford, crossed the Rapidan river, and camped at 11 P. M.

May 5th—Started early in the morning, and after a march of two hours brought up at Robertson's tavern, where we remained during the day. A great deal of fighting was going on that day within hearing, without much being gained on either side. A great many reports were flying about. From May 5th, '64, to May 20th, the great battle of the Wilderness was fought.

The dismounted men of the regiment guarded prisoners at Fredericksburg until May 21st, when they started for Bowling Green. The mounted portion of the Eighth New York Cavalry participated in the raid to Richmond; did their share of fighting and lost a number in killed, wounded and missing.

As the cavalry could not be used to any great advantage in the Wilderness, General Grant sent the third division of cavalry in the rear of General Lee's army to cut off his communications and stir up the Johnnies at Richmond; also at the same time make a flank movement to draw General Lee out of his fortified position. The expedition was commanded by the brave General Sheridan.

On the 6th of May the cavalry moved from Craig's Church to Spottsylvania Court House, where our cavalry struck the rebel cavalry, and had a fight with them May 8th. They drove them back and then moved on to Yellow Tavern, where our cavalry got up a lively fight, May 11th, and where the great cavalry leader, Rebel General Stuart was killed. The first Michigan brigade was on the advance that day and had the brunt of the battle.

Our cavalry moved on and had another brush with the rebels at Meadow Bridge the next day, and then pushed on to Richmond, burning depots and supplies on the way. The Union cavalry marched up in front of the fortifications around Richmond. The rebels began to fire away at our cavalry as soon as we were discovered, inflicting a loss of quite a number in killed and wounded, after which the Union cavalry withdrew and marched to Harrison's Landing, where they made a halt to rest the men and horses. Then they marched in the direction of Hanover Court House, crossing the Chickahominy, and making a detour around General Lee's whole army. The regiment participated in the battle of Hanover Court House, May 31st; Haines Shop, June 3d; White

Oak Swamp, June 13th; Malvern Hill, June 15th. Then came the great Wilson raid.

May 23d—The dismounted men, after receiving horses, marched to Bowling Green, and arriving at that place about 9 P. M., passed through the town, which is quite a village for Virginia, and turning to the right in the direction of Milford Station, bivouacked about mid-way between the two places.

May 24th—They marched to Milford Station, found the train, halted and drew three days' rations, after which we crossed the Matapony and marched to the right three miles, and went into camp in the woods. At this time Grant was driving Lee back towards Richmond and giving him gowdy.

May 27th—Marched to Milford Station.

May 28th—Started again at 3 P. M., and moved on through Newtown and halted.

May 30th—Started again about noon, crossed the Matapony and marched to Elliot. Kept moving until sundown. Grant hammering away at Lee yet.

May 31st—Marched to Pamunky river.

June 2d—Crossed the Pamunky river and camped. Grant made a successful flank movement and crossed the Chickahominy. Everything is lovely all along the line.

June 4th—The regiment in another fight. Colonel Benjamin and George Cook were wounded.

June 7th—Moved back to New Castle Ferry, the division doing picket duty.

June 9th—Drew three days' rations and started at

1 o'clock for White House Landing. Marched twelve miles and bivouacked for the night.

June 10th—Moved to White House Landing.

June 13th—The bugle routed us at 3 A. M., and at sunrise we started for the front. Crossed the Chickahominy below Bottom Bridge and marched six miles, found the brigade fighting, and went in. The regiment had quite a number wounded. Harry House, Corporal Crouswell and Sergeant Reed of Company H were wounded. Fell back after night and rode nearly all night.

June 14th—After two hours of sleep this morning, the regiment marched to near Harrison's Landing on the James river and grazed our horses.

June 15th—The regiment was on the advance this morning and moved in the direction of Haxall's Landing and Malvern Hill, and just before arriving at the latter place found the rebels and skirmished with them all day. We gradually fell back and at night bivouacked on the same ground which we occupied the night before. One man was killed in Company E, and several others wounded. Weather hot and dry.

June 16th—Lay in bivouac until half past seven, when we started in the direction of Charles City Court House. Drew one day's rations. There was no fighting in our vicinity that day.

June 17th—Up and ready to start at sunrise, marched to James river and crossed on a pontoon bridge. Lay around until 3 P. M., after which the regiment marched in the direction of Petersburg, about twelve miles, to Prince George Court House, where we bivouacked.

June 18th—Started at 5 o'clock and marched about two miles to the head waters of the Black Water and went into camp in the woods. Heavy cannonading in the direction of Petersburg.

June 21st—Had orders to get ready for ten days' active service. This was the commencement of the great Wilson raid in the southern part of Virginia.

June 22d—On the move early in the morning. Crossed the Petersburg & Weldon railroad, at Reams' Station, then marched to Dinwiddie Court House and on until we reached the Petersburg & Lynchburg railroad, following the same for about ten miles to Sutherland's Station, where we bivouacked for the night.

June 23d—On the move early in the morning, effectually destroying the depot with two locomotives and trains of cars at this station. The track was torn up for miles and fires built, burning the ties and heating the rails and bending them out of shape, thus rendering them unserviceable. As we passed along at Wilson, we burned the rebel barracks, and at Blacks and Whites burned three buildings containing cotton. On again towards the Junction. Ran upon the rebels at 2 P.M., and were fighting them for the remainder of the day. Burnett and Tennis Lowe, of Company H, were wounded.

June 24th—The regiment lay upon the skirmish

line last night. Were called in this morning, and the division on the move again. Heard that General Kautz was destroying the Junction, where we were fighting yesterday. Struck the Dansville railroad about noon, and followed it the remainder of the day, and bivouacked at night. Benjamin Curtis and Horace W. Sweet missing.

June 25th—Took a start early in the morning, following General Kautz, who has most effectually destroyed the railroad as he moved along. The rebels came up with our rear guard about 4 P. M., and were fighting them until dark, while General Kautz and the first brigade were engaging them near the railroad bridge across the Staunton river.

June 26th—Lay in support of the skirmishers until 2 o'clock this morning, when we moved on to Roanoake Station, where we left the railroad and took the road for Petersburg. Men and horses were pretty well tired out. Passed through Christianville to-day.

June 27th—Our regiment on the advance until we made a halt and dismounted. The most of the regiment was deployed as skirmishers to protect our left flank, which brought us in the rear during the after part of the day. Not much fighting to-day. Have to depend upon foraging for a living now.

June 28th—Came to Stony Creek to-day and crossed, with the expectation of having a big fight to-night or to-morrow.

June 29th—Fighting all last night near Stony Creek Station on the Petersburg & Weldon railroad, and this morning had to get up and dust out to save ourselves from being captured. The rebels came down onto the regiment with a large force and came near taking us all prisoners. They captured a large number of men. The most of us saved ourselves by putting spurs to our horses and scattering around the country, by running our horses and taking cross roads. Most of the regiment came up with the division at Reams' Station, where they were fighting. The rebels headed our cavalry off at that place, and we could not break through them. After burning the train, the cavalry turned south again. Then came one of the greatest get up and get marches that ever was known. Stephen Scott, Sidney Bowers and a number of others missing; George Camp and Herbert Hartson wounded.

June 30th—Marched all night at a break-neck gait and crossed the Weldon railroad early in the morning. Men and horses nearly played out. Crossed the Nottoway this afternoon.

July 1st—Marched all night again and crossed the Blackwater early this morning, and came within our lines, this forenoon, near Cabin Point. Halted about noon and rested for the remainder of the day. Men and horses all tired out.

That was the end of one of the greatest raids during the war. The men suffered untold hardships, travelled day and night, marching and fighting and tearing up railroad tracks, for ten days. It was thought at first that more than half of the regiment had been taken prisoners, but a large number wandered around for two days and finally got back to the regiment. Benjamin Curtis, Horace W. Sweet, George Camp, Herbert Hartson, Stephen Scott, James Bennett, Darwin H. Pierce, Theodore P. Whiting, John Burkhard, Gilbert Brown, of Company H, were taken prisoners and sent to Andersonville prison. A number died there. The rest were exchanged before the war was over.

This is the way Benjamin Curtis came to get out of the rebel prison:

Some time in the fall of '64, when the rebel officer was calling off the names of prisoners to be exchanged, he called a name and no one answered to it. Curtis saw his chance and spoke up, "Here," and took his place in the line. A great many prisoners got away sooner than they would have done by doing that. The man that the rebel officer called was too sick to be there.

Many of the men of the Eighth New York, who lived through the war and to get home, died a few years after, from the hardships of that raid. About one-quarter of the regiment was taken prisoners.

CHAPTER VII.

REBEL PRISON—SANITARY COMMISSION—PICKET—PRINCE GEORGE COURT HOUSE—SPRINGING OF MINES—CITY POINT—TRANSFERRED TO THE SHENANDOAH VALLEY—GUARDING A WAGON TRAIN—HALLSTOWN—INTO MARYLAND AGAIN—ACROSS THE POTOMAC RIVER INTO VIRGINIA—AT SHEPARDSTOWN FORD—SCOUTING.

ON the 2d of July the regiment moved to City Point. While there, on July 4th, the boys had a treat from the United States Sanitary Commission, such sundry articles as canned meats, canned fruits, dried apples, and a small taste of spirits. Tremendous hot weather, dry and dusty. The regiment stayed at City Point until the 19th. It took the men and horses quite a while to recruit up.

July 19th—The regiment broke camp a little past noon and moved to the left of Petersburg, across the Petersburg and Norfolk railroad, and bivouacked.

July 20th—Moved out upon picket in the direction of the Blackwater. Heavy cannonading in the direction of Petersburg last night.

The boys were awakened this morning by firing in the direction of our pickets. We dusted out, mounted our horses, and were soon on the spot where the firing was heard, and ascertained that a patrol of twelve men had been attacked by a squadron of rebels, and driven back with the loss of two men wounded and four missing of Company K. Nothing more transpiring we returned to the reserve and were relieved. Then returned to near our old camp on the James, and went into camp again. Terrible hot weather, dry and dusty, as usual.

The next day the picket line moved. One squadron on picket at Prince George Court House.

July 28th—We were relieved by the First Vermont Cavalry, and then moved back to our old camp, packed up and on the move again in the direction of Petersburg. The next morning found the regiment near the old picket ground, to the left of Petersburg, and had just dug our eyes open when we were brought to our feet by a succession of rapid reports, which we have since learned was caused by the springing of mines, and heavy cannonading. At the same time our infantry charged the rebel works, capturing a part of them, and also capturing a large number of prisoners. Later in the day the regiment was formed for the purpose of making an attack in our front, but for some reason, to us unknown, were not brought into action, and about 2 o'clock P. M. withdrew and encamped. The next day on picket again.

August 1st—Were relieved by the Eighteenth Pennsylvania Cavalry, and marched to the Blackwater near Lee's Mills, and went into camp.

August 2d—Remained in camp all day, two squadrons of the regiment on picket. Hot and dry. Water scarce.

August 3d—Colonel Benjamin in command of the regiment again. On the 5th of August the regiment was called in from picket about 11 o'clock in the night, and marched to a station on the Norfolk railroad, where the regiment bivouacked until daylight, then fed and saddled and moved to City Point and went into camp. Stayed there until August 8th.

August 8th—The regiment embarked on board the steamship John Rice, and anchored for the night.

August 9th—The ship started and went down the James river past Fortress Monroe, then up the Chesapeake Bay and ran up the Potomac about twenty miles and anchored for the night.

August 10th—The boat pulled out at sunrise and arrived at Liesboro at noon, where the regiment disbanded and went into camp.

The Third Cavalry Division, that to which the Eighth New York Cavalry belonged, and one other division of cavalry were transferred from near Petersburg to the Shenandoah Valley under Sheridan, in the month of August, '64, where they participated in some of the severest fights of the war.

August 12th—The regiment left Liesboro Point, just at night, passed through Washington, crossed chain bridge and bivouacked about three miles from Drainsville. The boys were disappointed in not being paid. They found plenty of green corn and were having a very good living. Here quite a number of recruits joined the regiment. Among them were Andrew J. Terwilliger with his recruits.

August 13th—Moved on to Drainsville and bivouacked again. Captain Compson's squadron was sent upon picket up the turnpike.

August 15th—The regiment was up at an early hour and started again, crossed Goose Creek and through Leesburg. The regiment was detailed as wagon guards that day. The wheel of the wagon that Enos Guile was guarding came off in some way, and he had to stop to fix it. He got behind the rest. After he got it fixed, they started on again, and went about two miles when it came off again. By this time it was dark, and they were so far in the rear that a squad of rebels came down on them and took Guile prisoner. The driver dug out and saved himself. The rebels took Guile's horse and arms from him, and told him to follow on. They had not gone far when Guile jumped behind some bushes and stopped. The rebels went on and left him. In a little while he started on in the direction of our cavalry and came up with them that night at Percysville, where the regiment had stopped for the night, minus his horse and equipment, but glad to get out of it as well as that.

August 16th—We started at an early hour and moved through Snicker's Gap, across the Shenandoah river, through Perryville, made a short halt, drew forage and rations, and then moved on in the direction of White Post, about three miles and bivouacked. Enos Guile got another horse that day, so he was all right again.

August 17th—We marched through White Post and around to Winchester, where the rebels came down and drove us about three miles in the direction of Summit Point.

August 18*th*—One squadron was on picket until 3 o'clock in the morning, when they moved down to Summit Point and went into camp.

August 19*th and* 20*th*—We were doing picket duty and foraging. The weather changed. The morning was rainy and wet.

August 21*st*—We were driven from Summit Point to Charlestown by the rebels, who came down upon u s with a heavy force of infantry. We found out that we were cut off from Charlestown by the direct front, and had to make a detour and came into that place by the Berryville Pike. Bivouacked at a late hour.

August 22*d*—We were driven from Charlestown to Hallstown. Saddled at 3 A. M., and at daylight, the rebels attacked us and forced the cavalry back upon the infantry, which we found in line of battle upon the heights around Hallstown. Here the regiment was camped so close to the 114th New York Volunteers, the Chenango County regiment, that many of the boys went and made them a visit, being acquainted with them, for some of the 114th New York went from Norwich, New York.

August 25*th*—Went out in the direction of Martinsburg and got up a fight and were driven back. Had some hard fighting that day. Sidney Briggs was taken prisoner. One squadron on picket that night.

August 26*th*—We started about midnight and crossed into Pleasant Valley and moved on to

Boonsboro, expecting that the rebels were crossing into Maryland again. A heavy rain that evening.

August 27th—Started from Boonsboro about noon and marched direct to Sharpsburg, then moved about two miles up the Hagertown Pike and went into camp and put out a picket line.

August 28th—Marched from Sharpsburg to Charlestown by the Sheperdstown Ford across the Potomac.

August 29th—In camp all day.

August 30th—Marched from Charlestown to Berryville; encountered no opposition that day.

August 31st—We were sent upon picket in the direction of Snicker's Gap. High living—green corn and honey.

September 1st—One squadron was sent in the direction of Winchester as a support to the Twenty-Second New York Cavalry. They were making a reconnoissance. Found the rebel pickets upon the Winchester and Ashby's Gap turnpike; after which the cavalry returned to the picket reserve.

CHAPTER VIII.

OPEQUAN CREEK—MOSBY—SURPRISED AT SNICKER'S GAP, '64—BATTLE OF WINCHESTER IN '64—CHESTER GAP—SKIRMISHING—MILLFORD — NEWMARKET GAP — HARRISBURG — STAUNTON—GENERAL CUSTER—PAID OFF—DRAWING RATIONS—MILL CREEK—COLUMBIA FURNACE—CEDAR CREEK—THE BATTLE OF CEDAR CREEK.

WE got an early start the second of September, and moved back towards Charlestown, and, after dark, back to Berryville.

September 3d—Went on a reconnoissance towards Front Royal, through Millwood and White Post. The Eighth New York Cavalry went within four miles of Front Royal and back to Millwood and bivouacked.

September 4th—Back to Berryville, where the regiment found fighting going on, in which the Johnnies got the worst of it. Two squadrons of our regiment were sent upon picket near Berryville.

September 6th—We were relieved from picket duty and came back to camp. A very rainy and disagreeable time.

September 7th—On a reconnoissance towards White Post and Winchester by the whole of the Third Division. Got up quite a fight within about four miles of Winchester, upon the west side of the Opequan creek. Our cavalry were driven back. The most of our squadron were out as flankers.

September 9th—The Fourth Squadron was on a scout to Snicker's Ferry and to the left. They took two Johnnies prisoners. On picket and relieved in the evening by the Second New York Cavalry.

September 11*th*—The rebels attempted to break into our camp in the evening, but it proved to be a failure. It was supposed to be some of Mosby's doings. Our squadron was on a scout again to-day, and brought in a citizen guerilla. The 13th and 14th in camp.

September 14*th*—A detail of the best men and horses was made, and instructed to hold themselves in readiness to move at a minute's notice.

September 15*th*—Inspection by the Division Inspector, after which a detail of the regiment went with Major Ford upon a scout. Another detail started the same evening for Ashby's Gap.

The men who went out on the scout last night came in this evening, the 16th, about dark. They all agree in one thing, and that is, they have been having a rough and serious time of it. Everything had gone well and they had made a good thing of it, until, from some as yet unexplained reason, they allowed themselves to be surprised while resting in Snicker's Gap, which resulted in several being killed and wounded and some taken prisoners. Company H lost eight horses. James Robinett was very badly wounded.

September 17*th*—Upon picket. This evening, several of the boys, who were taken prisoners in yesterday's affray, made their escape and came into camp all right. We were drawn off from picket duty with the expectation of moving, but did not. Thomas

Carr, Legard Norton and Benjamin Casper were sent to the dismounted camp.

September 19th—Were up at half past one and on the move at half past two in the direction of Winchester. The First Brigade of the Third Division came upon the rebels at daylight, and drove them from their position on the Opequan. Our infantry came up, when a fight commenced in earnest, which resulted in the rebels being put to rout, and sent skedaddling out of Winchester. The cavalry made a number of successful charges during the day, and bivouacked late at night at Kernstown. The Eighth New York Cavalry lost a few in killed, wounded and missing. A great and glorious day's work for the Union troops.

September 20th—Marched from Kernstown out toward Front Royal. Did some skirmishing, but no regular fighting to-day. Halted about noon and laid around until night and bivouacked.

September 21st—Up long before daylight and moved across the north branch of the Shenandoah, and at daylight charged across the south branch and drove the rebels through Front Royal, and back into the mountains in the vicinity of Chester Gap, where we bivouacked. Sergeant Van B. Crain wounded to-day.

September 22d—On the move along the mountain. The fourth squadron acted as rear guard. Skirmishing to-day by the Twenty-second New York Cavalry, and also by the first brigade upon our right. Bivouacked late at night in the vicinity of Milford.

September 23d—Moved back toward Strausburg and travelled the same ground over again in the evening, and bivouacked about midnight, only upon the other side of Milford.

September 24th—Marched from Milford to New Market Gap. Fighting by the first division. Bivouacked late at night.

September 25th—Through the gap to New Market, and from there to Harrisonburg. Bivouacked late at night again. No more rations or forage to be drawn while in the valley, by order.

September 26th—From Harrisonburg to Staunton, with the fourth squadron upon picket. A very hard march to-day.

September 27th—On picket until three o'clock P. M., then moved to Waynesboro.

September 28th—We laid around until sundown, when the rebels came down, flanked us, and drove us back toward Staunton. The Eighth New York and the Twenty-Second New York Cavalry were cut off, and had to make a long detour to get away from the rebels.

September 29th—After a hard night's march, we brought up at Bridgewater. We came through Staunton and took the mountain road which leads to Bridgewater, where we arrived about noon.

September 30th—Lay in camp until dark, when we moved over upon the turnpike. General Custer assumed command of the Third Division to-day. The boys liked General Custer, there was some get up and get to him. He used the saber a great deal, which the boys of the Eighth New York liked. They were at home with the saber. The rebels could not stand in front of the Eighth New York Cavalry when they made a charge upon them.

October 2d—Moved camp and commenced to unsaddle, but had to saddle up again as the rebels were reported to be advancing upon us.

October 3d—The regiment was paid. One squadron was sent to escort the paymaster back to Harrisonburg.

October 4th—Stayed at Harrisonburg last night, and brought the paymaster back with us this morning. Then we were sent upon picket. Drew rations of sugar, coffee, hard tack and bacon.

October 5th—Everything quiet to-day. We were relieved and came in from picket about dark and bivouacked.

October 6th—Saddled up and on the move at daylight. Crossed over to the mountain road, passed through Dayton, Turleytown and Rockingham, beyond which the regiment went into camp. Foraging and barn-burning the principal order of the day. The first brigade had some skirmishing in our rear to-day.

October 7th—The First Vermont Cavalry was rear guard to-day. The rebels came down upon us at Mill Creek and drove the rear guard back upon the Eighth New York pell mell, breaking it, which gave the Johnnies a chance to "Give us Jesse," which they improved and drove us about half a mile, when the regiment rallied and stopped them. Sergeant Joseph Beadle was wounded. Marched to Columbia Furnace and halted for the night.

October 8th—The boys from dismounted camp came to the regiment to-day. The rebels pressing upon our rear, we moved about twelve miles and halted for the night.

October 9th—Up early in the morning and started after the Johnnies. Found them, attacked and drove them about five miles and took six pieces of artillery and seventy-five prisoners. Came back well satisfied with our day's work. The Eighth New York on picket that night.

October 11th—"Boots and saddles" was sounded about 1 P. M., after which we moved over upon the pike through Strausburg, across Cedar Creek and bivouacked.

October 13th—Sent upon picket at 10 o'clock. At 12 o'clock the rebels came down and drove the third New Jersey Cavalry from the ford above us, but at sundown, the Jersey boys were back at the ford again. Fighting to our left upon the pike.

October 14th—Came in from picket and made a new camp just at evening. No disturbance to-day.

October 16th—A row among the pickets all last night. "Boots and saddles" at half-past four this morning. Our regiment on a reconnoissance across Cedar Creek, but discovered nothing of the rebels.

October 17th—We were aroused from our slumbers long before daylight with "Boots and saddles," caused by a commotion among the pickets, which we afterwards ascertained, was caused by the rebels charging into and capturing one of our picket reserve belonging to the First Connecticut Cavalry. The Eighth New York was sent out about 10 o'clock, and established a new picket.

October 19th—"Boots and saddles," at 4 o'clock A. M. It was soon ascertained that the pickets upon our right were attacked and driven in. Soon after heavy firing upon our left gave us to understand that our infantry had been attacked also.

The result of the day's work may be summed up as follows: Sheridan's army was surprised and routed into a lively retreat which was checked by the efficiency of our cavalry corps. Our lines reformed, the rebels were routed and driven in disorder back across Cedar Creek. Several pieces of artillery were captured by the First Vermont and the Fifth New York Cavalry.

On the 19th of October, 1864, the great battle of Cedar Creek was fought. Lee sent Longstreet with his corps to reinforce Early. While Sheridan was away, Rebel General Early took the opportunity to attack the Union Army. The rebels managed to capture some of the Union pickets, and marched through and surprised the Union camp about 4 o'clock A. M. Before the Union troops could be rallied, the rebels captured a large number of prisoners, and sent the rest flying. Then the cavalry stepped in between the flying Union Army and the rebels and checked them.

About noon General Sheridan arrived on the field. Then the infantry were formed in position. General Sheridan says: "We are going the other way." Soon an advance was made and the tide turned the other way. The rebels were sent flying back. When night came, the Rebel Army was completely demoralized. About fifty pieces of artillery were captured and several thousand prisoners.

The cavalry saved the battle of Cedar Creek. They will never get their just dues for what they did at that battle. B. W. Wilson, Colonel of the Twenty-Eighth Iowa, says in his account of the battle: "If it had not been for the cavalry, the army would have been driven back to Winchester."

October 20th—Saddled up early and started on a reconnoissance to the front. Advanced as far as Fisher's Hill, but meeting with no opposition, returned to camp late in the evening.

CHAPTER IX.

PICKET DUTY--SCOUTING--FISHER'S HILL--RETREAT--RECONNOISSANCE BY MOONLIGHT—MOUNT JACKSON—WINTER WEATHER—CROSSING CEDAR CREEK—FORAGING—RECONNOITERING—WOODSTOCK—THE REBELS CHARGE ON OUR BRIGADE—DRIVING THE REBELS BACK—CHRISTMAS—GOOD NEWS FROM SHERMAN'S ARMY—WINTER QUARTERS—EXECUTION OF TWO DESERTERS BELONGING TO THE THIRD NEW YORK CAVALRY—EXPLOITS OF A CAVALRYMAN IN CAMP—SKIRMISHING—ON THE MARCH—WAYNESBORO—CHARGING THE REBELS' BREASTWORKS—A GREAT FEAT—REBEL GENERAL EARLY—REBEL PRISONERS—TYE RIVER—BURNING RAILROAD BRIDGES.

MOVED camp about noon, October 21st, 1864. Drew two days' rations, one day's forage, and then were sent upon picket at Cupp's Mills, on Cedar Creek.

October 22d—Company H, having been on picket by themselves during the night, came in and found two recruits for the company, Samuel Williams and Richard Cole. The regiment did picket duty in that vicinity until the 29th.

October 29th—The regiment was sent to Woodstock upon a reconnoissance. Returned about 3 o'clock P. M.

October 30th—Mounted inspection at 10 o'clock, after which we put up a picket line for our horses.

October 31st—All the boys who had not re-enlisted left the regiment.

November 3d—The regiment was consolidated into eight companies.

November 5th—Spent the forenoon in changing quarters, after which a detail was made to go foraging. Went about eight miles and returned about sundown. Upon reaching camp, we were ordered not to unsaddle, but to get ready to go immediately in light marching order. Two squadrons of our regiment, a part of the First Vermont and a portion of the Second New York Cavalry, moved to Newtown in the night, where we remained saddled, and at daylight on the morning of the 6th, pushed on as far as White Post, but failing to find the rebels, came back to camp again, arriving there about noon.

November 7th—Called up at half past four, and at daylight the Eighth and Twenty-Second New York Cavalry moved out, crossed Cedar Creek and advanced beyond Fisher's Hill. They failed to find the enemy and returned to camp again.

November 8th—Saddled and packed for a move, but unsaddled and put up our quarters again. Part of the division on a scout.

November 9th—Sent upon picket in the afternoon in the direction of the front.

November 10th—After being changed about from one reserve to another, we finally got back to our company about midnight, where we remained until daylight, when the cavalry fell back to within three miles of Winchester, went into camp and drew rations.

November 11th—Moved camp and worked hard, putting up a picket line for our horses, until half past two o'clock. We had scarcely finished, when the rebels attacked our pickets and drove them back upon the infantry line of the same. Saddled and got out as quickly as possible and had quite a skirmish, which resulted in stopping the rebels. Company D had two men wounded in the fight.

Made a reconnoissance the same night by moonlight. Came upon the rebel pickets, charged them, captured two of them and returned to camp at midnight.

November 12*th*—Saddled again before daylight. The rebels attacked our lines again about 8 A. M. Near noon we got down to business and had a big cavalry fight, charging and recharging. John Kehoe was wounded. On picket to-night.

November 13*th*—A squad of men were sent out at 1 o'clock A. M. to help the First New Hampshire on the left of our line. Were called in about 10 o'clock, after which the division made a reconnoissance as far as Cedar Creek. No rebels met with. On picket again at night.

November 14*th*—Remained on picket until dark, when we were relieved by the First Vermont Cavalry, and returned to camp about 8 o'clock, after which the regiment drew rations and forage.

November 17*th*—The second squadron was sent upon picket at the Carter mansion.

November 18*th*—Were relieved from picket at noon by the First New Hampshire Cavalry and came into camp.

November 19*th*—Lay in camp all day. Received

orders to be ready for inspection the next day at 10 A. M. The weather cold and rainy.

November 20th—Sunday. A rainy day, therefore there was no inspection.

November 21st—Were called up at 5 o'clock, and ordered to be ready to move. Moved at daylight and marched to Woodstock and bivouacked in the midst of a pelting rain.

November 22d—Saddled before daylight and the column commenced to move soon after. The division commanded by General Powell on the advance. At Mount Jackson encountered Early's force of infantry and cavalry, and after a severe fight of a few hours, fell back to Woodstock, where we bivouacked for the night. The second squadron on picket. Very cold and windy.

November 23d—Took an early start and arrived in camp about 3 o'clock P. M. Weather very cold and a great amount of suffering caused by it on the march.

November 26th—The second and fourth squadrons were sent to Stephenson's Depot for train guard. Returned to camp at 10 P. M.

November 27th—Sunday. Had mounted inspection by General Custer, after which we put up a picket line for our horses.

November 28th—After breakfast had "Boots and saddles," and went upon a reconnoissance across Cedar Creek and on through the mountain to Wardensville, on the Capon river. Moved back about three miles and bivouacked about 10 o'clock P. M., after a hard march of about thirty miles.

November 29th—Were getting ready to return to camp when the balance of the division came along and we fell in with the column and made a march through the mountains, crossing Lost river valley and up the mountain again fifteen miles or more and bivouacked. No rations except what we foraged.

November 30th—On the march at daylight this morning, and reached Mooresfield, twelve miles, at 11 A. M. Fed our horses, got our dinner, and did some foraging. Commenced moving back about 4 P. M. Bivouacked near the same locality that we did the preceding night, but upon another road.

December 1st—On the move early again, through a very mountainous country. The Eighth New York Cavalry on the advance. Made a halt of about an hour in a beautiful valley, the name of which we did not learn, then moved on and bivouacked near Capon bridge across Capon river.

December 2d—Moved out early again, through the mountains and arrived in camp about 3 o'clock P. M., having marched, during the past five days, over one hundred and twenty miles.

December 3d—Remained in camp all day. The weather cold but pleasant.

December 4th—The regiment was sent upon picket near the Carter House. A detail of the regiment went on a reconnoissance to Cedar Creek, but returned to camp about noon without having discovered any signs of the enemy.

December 6th—In camp at work upon winter quarters. The Fifteenth New York Cavalry joined the brigade last evening. Pleasant weather.

December 9th—A cold day. Had to saddle up at 10 o'clock, and reconnoitre as far as Copp's Mills, on Cedar Creek. Our squadron crossed the creek and advanced a mile, but discovered no signs of the rebels. Returned to camp about half past four in the morning. A very cold night for reconnoissance. Nothing of importance going on to-day.

December 10th—About six inches of snow fell last night and this morning. Saddled at 9 o'clock, A. M. In reserve upon the middle road.

December 11th—Were sent to Cupp's Mills on a reconnoissance. Started at 5 o'clock in the morning, and returned at 9 o'clock A. M. Were relieved about noon and returned to camp. Randall J. Beadle, John Kehoe and Nathan Bowen came to the company to-day. The prospect bids fair for an extremely cold night.

December 12th—About the coldest morning that has been experienced during the war. Our rations small for man and beast. To-day each man was provided with a new forage cap. Letter of his company, cross sabers and the number of his regiment are on them, and he is required to wear the same. Worked hard all day on our quarters. A great moderation in the weather since yesterday.

December 15th—In camp to-day and finished our shanties.

December 16th—In camp again to-day. A great salute fired in honor of a great battle. It is reported that General Thomas has whipped Hood at Marshville.

December 17th—A part of the regiment was sent upon picket. The news of General Thomas' victory confirmed, and a salute of one hundred guns fired in honor of it.

December 18th—Were sent upon picket this morning, on the back road. Rainy to-day.

December 19th—Were called into camp about 10 o'clock last night, and received orders to get everything ready to break camp at daylight this morning. We broke camp agreeable to the above order, and marched to Woodstock and bivouacked. A mild rain through the day.

December 20th—Up at an early hour, got our breakfast, and at daylight on the march again. At Mount Jackson, several dispatches from General Sheridan were read to us, after which we moved on through New Market, and about eight miles beyond there, and then bivouacked. Pleasant weather for the season.

December 21st—It commenced to rain in the night, and after a little it commenced to snow, making it very disagreeable packing this morning. Up at 4 o'clock and had everything in readiness to move at 6. Were mounted and had commenced moving out, when the rebels charged into our brigade and drove us about half a mile. But rallying, we drove them, inflicting a very heavy loss upon them in killed, wounded and prisoners, after which we moved back to Woodstock. Edward Bensing wounded this morning.

December 22d—The weather grew colder all of last night, and during our march back to Winchester to-day. The men suffered severely from the extreme cold. Arrived at Camp Russell about 3 o'clock P. M., and went into camp in a new place. About the hardest marching for horses that we have ever experienced, it being very slippery. The Eighth New York was in the rear to-day, and our squadron was rear guard until we reached Cedar Creek, when we were relieved by Captain Hamilton's squadron.

December 23d—In camp. · The weather cold, but not as tedious as yesterday.

December 24th—A change in the weather; warmer. A dismounted inspection by the Brigade Inspector.

December 25th—Christmas. Sunday inspection, but no turkey.

December 26th—Good news from Sherman, in the capture of Savannah.

December 28th—Had orders to be ready to move at 10 o'clock A. M.

December 29th—A cold morning. Moved out of camp agreeable to orders, marched through Winchester, up the Romeny pike, and encamped in a piece of woods. Received orders to put up a corral for our horses, and to build winter quarters. Like the situation of our camp well.

December 30th—Put up a corral and worked at our shanties. Cold weather yet.

December 31st—Cold and stormy. Worked upon our quarters.

January 1st, 1865—Dismounted company inspection by Company Commander this forenoon. At work upon our quarters again to-day. Weather cold.

January 2d—Moved into our shanties to-day.

January 3d—The first and part of the second squadron sent upon picket. Pleasant morning, but stormy towards evening.

January 4th—Experienced a very rough and tedious night upon picket. Were relieved by our own regiment, and came into camp about noon. Weather cold and blustering. Worked fixing up our shebangs.

January 6th—Saddled at 10 o'clock A. M., and moved out to division headquarters to witness the execution of two men belonging to the Third New York Cavalry. The crime was desertion and attempting to carry information to the enemy.

January 8th—Inspection, dismounted, by Sergeant Walter B. Norton, commanding company.

January 9th—In camp and not much going on. Pleasant day. Slicked up our camp.

We camped at that place until February 26th. About all that was going on was picket duty, inspections, reviews and regular camp duty.

Some people think that there is no hard work about soldiering. I will tell you what a cavalryman has to do when in camp. The first thing after he gets up is to attend to his horse. He feeds his horse his grain, consisting of oats and corn mixed together, which is drawn from the government. The horse eats his grain out of a nose bag, which is held on by a strap that goes over his head like a halter. While he is eating we have to groom him one hour. Not fifty-nine minutes, but sixty full minutes, and keep busy all the time. There is an officer watching you all this time, and if you stop he yells out: " Keep to work there!" After that the boys get their breakfast, having to cook it themselves. Then comes watering horses. Sometimes a man has to go quite a ways. Guard mounting for camp guard follows. Then your equipments have to be kept clean. A cavalryman has more equipments than any other branch of the service; a saber, carbine and revolver. The cavalry is the hardest branch there is in the service. When it comes night we have our horses to water and feed again. In fact, a cavalryman is kept busy all day long. I almost forgot to say that a soldier has something to do to keep clear from " greybacks." When a soldier is on duty, some one is detailed to take care of his horse, so that most every man has two horses to take care of. This is when soldiers are in camp. When we are at the front, or on the march, or fighting the rebels, it is different. There is not so much red tape then.

When we are in camp we have inspection every Sunday, and if there is any rust on our equipments, or if they are not clean, and if the soldier is not clean, or his clothes, he is sent to his quarters and given so long a time to get them in order. And it has to be done. Most always the soldier is in trim on the inspection, for he knows that he would be sent back again.

February 26th—Division review to-day, and had orders to break camp at 6 o'clock to-morrow morning.

February 27th—On the move at daylight. The first and third divisions, with one brigade of the second division, compose our force in motion. Marched to Woodstock and bivouacked. Cold weather yet.

February 28th—Advanced from Woodstock to Lacy's Springs. Our company on picket this evening. Not much sign of the rebels to-day.

March 1st—Marched from Lacy's Springs to within about six miles of Staunton, the advance guard skirmishing with a small force of the enemy all day.

March 2d—It commenced raining at daylight and kept it up all day. We passed through Staunton and on to Waynesboro, where we found the enemy in position. Threw out skirmishers and were drawn up in line when the rebels opened upon us with their artillery, which was well served and proved rather destructive to us. After waiting about an hour, we charged the rebels. The Eighth New York was ordered to lead the charge, a thing which they had done before. They were almost always the first in a fight and the last to leave it. The enemy was completely routed and demoralized, and driven across the river. Rebel General Early barely escaped capture, he having had his horse shot under him by Major Compson, who was commanding the Eighth New York at that time.

The Eighth New York Cavalry accomplished that day the greatest feat on record. They charged over the rebels' breastworks, mounted, and captured eight hundred prisoners, which was nearly twice their number, five pieces of artillery, a large number of wagons and ambulances, several portable blacksmith forges, many hundred stands of small arms, several sets of single harness, many hundred horses and mules, and a number of battle flags, before the support came up, something that was never done by the same number of men during the rebellion.

The regiment marched through Rockfish Gap and bivouacked late at night. Henry Carr was killed by a shell, and John Kehoe, of Company H, wounded to-day.

March 3d—Marched from Brooksville to Charlottsville. Very muddy traveling.

March 4th—Saddled before daylight. One squadron was sent upon picket this afternoon, and remained until 10 o'clock P. M., when we were relieved by the Fifteenth New York Cavalry, and joined the regiment.

March 6th—On the move again in the direction of Lynchburg. Bivouacked near Rockfish river. Muddy marching. Passed through a mountainous but beautiful country, having to depend upon the country for forage and rations.

March 7th—Marched from Rockfish river to Tye river, and burned the railroad bridge across that stream. Weather pleasant and no enemy to oppose us yet.

CHAPTER X.

BUFFALO RIVER—SCOTTSVILLE—COLUMBIA—FREDERICK'S HALL—BEAVER DAM STATION—SOUTH ANNA—NORTH ANNA—MATAPONY—PAMUNKEY RIVER—FIVE FORKS—THE CAVALRY CHARGE—SOUTH SIDE RAILROAD—CAPTURE OF RICHMOND—APPOMATTOX STATION—FLAG OF TRUCE—CLOSE OF THE WAR—GENERAL CUSTER'S REMARKS—TRIP TO WASHINGTON—GRAND REVIEW—POST OF HONOR—CUSTER'S COMPLIMENT—CUSTER'S FAREWELL—BACK INTO VIRGINIA AGAIN—DRILLING—HOMEWARD BOUND—THE FINAL DISCHARGE.

CROSSED Tye river March 8th, and advanced to Buffalo river, where we burned the railroad bridge and then crossed over to New Market upon the James river, and joined the rest of the corps. Moved from New Market to Scottsville, and bivouacked about 8 o'clock P. M., from Scottsville to Columbia, where we arrived about 3 P. M., and went into camp. Laid in camp with the exception of foraging, till the 12th of March, when we marched to Frederick's Hall, and captured a few prisoners. The brigade busy tearing up railroad track this evening.

March 13th—Tearing up railroad in the forenoon, and on the move in the afternoon. The Eighth New York Cavalry and part of the First Vermont Cavalry were sent to Beaver Dam Station in the evening; ran across a few rebels, and had a little skirmishing on the way. Company D on picket to-night. Pleasant weather.

March 14th—Made a hard march and reached Squirrel bridge on the South Anna. Crossed and bivouacked. Had a little trouble on picket this morning.

March 15th—On the move early in the morning, re-crossed the river, then countermarched across the river again, then to Ashland. Found the enemy in force. Moved back toward Hanover Junction, crossed the South Anna again. Made a halt of a few hours, and at dark once more on the road. We crossed the North Anna at Oxford, and bivouacked very late.

March 16th—Moved about twenty miles towards Azlitts' Landing and went early into camp.

March 17th—Advanced ten miles to Azlitts' Landing on the Matapony, then to King William Court House and bivouacked.

March 18th—Marched to the White House Landing, where we went into camp about noon.

March 19th—Crossed the Pamunky and went into camp. Drew rations and sent out a scout this afternoon.

March 21st—Ten men of Company D with our arms and horses' equipments, took passage on the steamboat *Ella* for City Point. The night was very wet and windy. Lay upon deck and took a soaking.

March 22d—Reached Fortress Monroe about noon, having experienced a very rough passage. The sea was so rough that we could not get to the wharf to take in coal, and the result was that we had to pass the night at anchor.

March 23d—At daylight moved up to the wharf

to take in coal, and lay there until the next morning, being unable to get off.

March 24th—Weighed anchor at daylight and reached City Point at 5 P. M. Disembarked and went into camp about one mile from City Point. A big battle was in progress between here and Petersburg. The boys from Company D on special duty, were: Laguard Norton, Walter B. Norton, Edwin A. Miner, Lee Spoor, Hiram Shippey, John I. Littler, Frank Eggleston, Samuel Williams, Dana Guile and Enos Guile.

March 29th—Walter B. Norton, Laguard Norton, Samuel Williams and Frank Eggleston left for the front.

The army on the move again. General Sheridan with the cavalry corps and three corps of infantry marched his army around the right flank of the Rebel Army, after passing over some of the worst roads that were ever known.

April 1st—The Second Brigade, to which the Eighth New York Cavalry belonged, made a charge upon the rebels, who were behind breastworks near Five Forks. The brigade was repulsed twice, but on the third charge the boys went in so heavy the rebels could not stand before them. They went flying in all directions, followed by our cavalry, which captured a number of them. The Eighth New York Cavalry suffered severely and lost their color-bearer, Nathan Bowen, who was killed, and a number who were wounded. Some of the latter died from the effects of their wounds.

April 2d—Heavy cannonading last night, which has been kept up nearly all day. Encouraging news from the front of Petersburg and the left of our lines. Sheridan in possession of the South Side railroad, and thousands of prisoners captured.

April 3d—Petersburg and Richmond in possession of the Union Army. Such rejoicing never was known before. The soldiers yelled and hurrahed, the gunboats fired salutes, and salutes were fired everywhere, echoing and re-echoing over the hills and through the valleys. Sheridan with his cavalry pressed on after the flying rebels and engaged them at every opportunity.

April 8th—Sheridan took his cavalry, and making a rapid detour from our left flank, got ahead of the Rebel Army at Appomattox Station, just at night, and checked Lee's army, capturing a large number of pieces of artillery. During the night, by forced marches, the infantry came up. The next morning Lee ordered a charge. But the cavalry, moving aside, revealed large bodies of infantry in battle line.

The civil war was about to close. General Grant had already demanded the surrender of the Confederate Army. During the day, a flag of truce was received by the Eighth New York Cavalry, which was at the front.

April 9th—General Lee surrendered what was left of the army of Virginia, near Appomattox Court House. This closed the war.

Then there was more rejoicing all over the North, East and West.

Remarks of General Custer, April 9th, 1865, when the war ended and the task of the historian began:

"When those deeds of daring, which have rendered the name and fame of the Third Cavalry Division imperishable, are inscribed upon the bright pages of our country's history, I only ask that my name may be written as that of the commander of the Third Cavalry Division.

G. A. CUSTER,
Brevet Major-General Commanding.

After the surrender of Lee's army, the cavalry was sent south to help Sherman. Near Halifax Court House a messenger met them, who bore the news that General Johnston had surrendered, when the cavalry turned back.

April 13th—Ordered to be ready to leave camp at 7 o'clock to-morrow morning, all that are mounted and equipped.

April 14th—Left camp. Marched through Petersburg and along the South Side railroad to Sunderland's station, near which we bivouacked about 6 P. M. All tired and hungry to-night.

April 15th—It commenced to rain before daylight and kept it up until near noon. Moved to Ford's Station and bivouacked about noon.

April 17th—Moved to Wilson Station and bivouacked.

April 18th—Marched to within two miles of Petersburg and into camp.

April 20th—Moved about two miles and went into camp again.

April 24th—Moved out upon the Boydton plank road to Nottoway bridge and bivouacked about 9 o'clock P. M. The weather was dry and dusty.

April 25th—On the road again in the direction of Boydton. Bivouacked to-night near the river.

April 26th—On the march again at 8 A. M. Moved up the river about five miles, forded it and came upon the plank road again, followed it to Boydton, where we bivouacked.

April 27th—Marched through a very fine looking country to Mecklingburg on the Staunton River, crossed and marched about six miles and bivouacked.

April 28th—Not a very early start, but marched rather fast for about twenty miles, when it was ascertained that Rebel General Johnston had surrendered; whereupon we halted and went into camp about 3 o'clock P. M., and bivouacked near Halifax Court House. Later in the day crossed the Richmond & Dansville railroad. Dry and dusty travelling.

April 29th—Moved from our bivouack to Staunton river at Mosley's Ferry, crossed and bivouacked near Roanoake station. A heavy thunder storm just after dark.

April 30th—Pleasant morning. A late start and a march of about twenty-five miles through Keysville, and bivouacked soon after dark.

May 1st—Moved earlier than common, and made Blacks and Whites at sundown. The thunder shower last night made it cooler and better travelling to-day.

May 2d—Made a very good haul on horse feed this morning. Marched to near Ford's Station and bivouacked. Drew rations of pork and hard tack. Weather pleasant.

May 3d—Arrived at Petersburg about noon, marched through the streets by sections, crossed the Appomattox and went into camp.

May 6th—In camp all day, expect the corps will start for Washington soon. Rumors upon rumors floating about camp as to the future of this regiment.

May 7th—Sunday morning, dismounted inspection by companies. Preaching by our new chaplain. In camp yet and warm.

May 9th—Drilled to-day. Colonel Pope assumed command of the regiment.

May 10th—Left Petersburg, marched through Richmond and bivouacked about five miles from the latter place at 6 P. M., on the road towards Squirrel bridge on the South Anna.

May 11th—Very warm. Made a good march of over thirty-five miles in the direction of Louisa Court House. Crossed the South Anna at Squirrel bridge. Thunder showers in the evening.

May 12th—Cool morning and not a very early start, but made a good day's march, crossed the North Anna and bivouacked about sundown.

May 13th—Did not get on the move very early, made Raccoon Ford on the Rapidam at sundown, crossed and bivouacked. Pleasant and warm.

May 14th—The third division on the advance to-day from Raccoon Ford to Kelley's, on the Rappahannock, thence to Catlitt's Station, and turned in for the night.

May 15th—The Eighth New York in the rear of everything to-day. Late to start, but were into camp at Fairfax Court House at 6 P. M. Pleasant to-day, but rather too dusty to be agreeable marching.

May 16th—Marched from Fairfax Court House, through Alexandria and camped.

May 20th—Ordered to be ready to move at 8 o'clock A. M., but after packing and remaining in line until 10 o'clock, were ordered into camp again. Drew rations of coffee, sugar, pork and bread.

May 21st—Ordered to be ready to move at 7 o'clock, A. M., moved about 9 o'clock, crossed Long bridge and past General Sheridan's headquarters, back upon Pennsylvania Avenue, past the Capitol; then took the Blandensburg pike on through Blandensburg about two miles, and into the woods and encamped. Rainy and muddy.

May 22d—Dismounted inspection by the brigade inspector, drew clothing to be ready for the grand review to-morrow at 4 o'clock A. M. Warm day.

May 23d—Up at 3 o'clock, "Boots and saddles" at 4 o'clock, on the move at 5 o'clock, at the Capitol at 8, and then commenced the great parade at 9. Passed through Washington by platoons by the way of Pennsylvania Avenue, after which our division formed and took farewell leave of General Custer. Then took up our line of march and arrived in camp about 3 P. M. The dismounted men and recruits joined us to-day. The Eighth New York Cavalry was awarded the post of honor at the great review, they being the advance regiment in that great march. There being a crook in Pennsylvania Avenue, opposite the U. S. Treasury Building, it was necessary to make a half right and left wheel. So straight did the men make the movement, that if any one had drawn a straight line across the breasts of the men it would not have varied a hair.

After the review the regiment marched into a side street and formed in line while General Custer took farewell leave of the division. The brave General Custer when he came along, paid the Eighth New York Cavalry this great compliment:

"Soldiers of the Eighth New York: I have orders to leave for Texas immediately. I wanted to take you with me, but I have no order to that effect.

"Men of the Eighth New York, you are the best soldiers I ever saw."

The tears began to flow down his cheeks.

"Good by."

He wheeled his horse and put spurs to him, and was soon out of sight.

There were more people assembled in Washington that day, than was ever known before or since at one time.

May 27th—"Boots and saddles" at 5 o'clock, but had not saddled, when the order was countermanded. Expect to move back into Virginia again.

May 29th—Broke camp at 6 o'clock A. M., marched rough Washington across Long bridge, through

Alexandria and up the pike about four miles and encamped.

June 2d—Inspection of the mounted and dismounted men this afternoon by the same Major from Washington. Very hot weather.

June 5th—Drill to-day. A charge on the sutler last night, and two men shot. Drew rations of coffee, sugar, etc.

June 8th—Lee, Littler, Sweet and W. J. Manning left the regiment with their discharges. Happy men. At work upon a bower for the government horses. Hot with a refreshing shower in the afternoon.

June 11th—A long and tedious inspection dismounted, by Colonel Pope.

June 14th—Drill in the forenoon by Colonel Bliss.

June 18th—Dismounted inspection by company commanders. An order came for the muster out of the regiment. Great rejoicing. Dress parade at 5 P. M.

June 25th—Up at 4 o'clock, got breakfast, broke camp at 5, and marched to a station on the Orange and Alexandria railroad, took the cars, reached Washington about 8 o'clock. Changed cars and left Washington at half past eleven; arrived in Baltimore about 4 P. M., where they gave us a dinner. Boarded the cars again at 8 for Elmira, by the Southern Central railroad.

June 26th—The boys passed a very uncomfortable night on the cars, they being freight cars and packed to their utmost capacity. Reached Williamsport at dark, and arrived at Elmira at daylight.

June 27th—Took breakfast, and at noon boarded the train again for Rochester, where we arrived at 8 o'clock P. M.

It is down on record that the regiment was mustered out June 27th, 1865, but many of the boys never got their discharge and pay until July 11th and 12th. Some went home before the 4th and went back again to Rochester for their discharges.

Comrades, it has been nearly twenty-four years since the war closed. The most of us have never seen each other since we separated. A large number have answered to their last roll call. Future generations will never know what the soldiers suffered in the War of the Rebellion. Comrades, how often do you think of those who gave up their lives for their country?

The author has written a history for the benefit of the officers and members of the Eighth New York Volunteer Cavalry, and to bring back to their memory the soldier days when we used to march and fight side by side in the great struggle for the Union. Every survivor must have a correct history of the regiment to hand down, before it is too late. We are not going to stay here always. If there is not some record of the deeds we did in the war, they will soon pass away and no one can tell what we did to put down the rebellion and that he fought in the Eighth New York Cavalry.

Many thanks to the comrades who have aided me in preparing this history. Long life and prosperity to the comrades of the Eighth New York Cavalry and all veterans of the war.

Three cheers for the " Red, White and Blue!"

Long may it wave,
O'er the land of the free
And the home of the brave!

The record of the Eighth New York Volunteer Cavalry beats them all.

COMMUNICATIONS FROM COMRADES.

ADVENTURES OF COMRADE EARL W. SOPER AT THE BATTLE OF MINE RUN.

LATE in the fall of the year 1863, after the battle of Gettysburg, the Army of the Potomac lay in camp on the north side of the Rapidan river, Va. The cavalry corps under General Pleasanton occupied a position near Culpepper Court House. The rebel army under General Lee occupied the south side of the Rapidan, in the wilderness near Mine Run.

The soldiers of our regiment, the Eighth New York Cavalry, were busily engaged in preparing for winter, notwithstanding the officers gave us no encouragement to build winter quarters. But we had laid in camp some time, and it was getting late in the season; therefore we felt safe in making the necessary preparation without orders, as usual. In looking from an officer's standpoint, it would seem as though we were expected to resume the march at any moment. Finally, on the 26th of November, we broke camp by orders from headquarters and took up the line of march in the direction of the Rapidan river. At that time I did not know the nature or destination of the movement, being only a private soldier in the ranks; and in fact I believe I would have avoided asking if I had known that I could have found out. Company M and Company D, of the Eighth New York, the former of which I was a member, were detailed to lead the advance of the Third Corps, General French.

The Third Army Corps crossed the Rapidan as follows: The Second Corps, General Warren, crossed at Germinia Ford, taking the road to Orange Court

House via. Robertson's Tavern; The Third Corps, General French, at Jacob's Mills Ford and took position on the right of the Second Corps; the Fifth Corps, General Sykes, at Culpepper Ford towards the Fredericksburg plank road and formed a junction with the Second Corps on its right at the forks of the road at Robertson's Tavern; the Sixth Corps, General Sedgwick, followed the Third Corps at Jacob's Mills Ford, and the First Corps, General Newton, with the reserve artillery and wagon trains, followed the Fifth Corps across Culpepper Ford.

The country on the north side of the Rapidan for a considerable distance is quite level, at least this is the case at Jacob's Mills Ford where we crossed; while the opposite shore is high and bluffy and cut up more or less by deep ravines, giving the enemy's pickets, as their advanced posts were along the south shore of the Rapidan, a full view of our columns long before we reached the river. As we approached, the rebels left their posts without firing their guns, and our little squad, Company M and D, dashed across on the bluffs without opposition and there waited for several hours for the infantry. The water was about waist high, and the soldiers forded the river, there being no pontoons at hand.

We marched a short distance on the road leading towards Chancellorsville, then we bore gradually to the right on the road leading to Locust Grove in the Wilderness. The road was just a narrow passageway, scarcely wide enough for four horses to walk abreast. After marching up to within about a half mile of the Orange Court House plank road, we came to a little cleared field on the left of the road, with an old log cabin near the center. Here the columns halted for some cause, I did not learn at the time, but afterwards I was informed that we were slightly lost. Our little band, Companies M and D, were some thirty or forty rods in the advance of the infantry. After standing here for some time waiting for orders to move, and none coming, the soldiers became restless and they broke ranks, took possession of the field, stacked their arms, built fires, and made all preparations for a general camp for the day, as though there was not a rebel within forty miles of us, when the enemy was actually within a few hundred feet of us, concealed by the dense wilderness.

According to military tactics during the war, Companies M and D being the advance guard, remained in the saddle until further orders. Time moved along slowly, as I always felt better in such places of expected danger when under motion. Finally Captain Niven, of Company M, and Captain Ford, of Company D, made a short reconnoissance to the front. In a few minutes they returned, and by their request we formed line and counted off in low tones. My number was twelve. Captain Niven told me in a suppressed voice that I should cross the Orange Court House plank road, about a-half or three-quarters of a mile ahead, and take a path on the other side of the plank road opposite of the road we were then on, and follow it until I came to where the path forked. Here I was to stay until relieved and watch the movements of seven or eight rebel soldiers about one-half a mile distant, over a broad and shallow ravine covered with underbrush, but not so tall but what I could see over the top to the cleared land beyond where the rebels stood, down the right hand fork of this path. Captain Niven also said that several of the soldiers would accompany me as far as the Orange Court House plank road, and there they would remain as a reserve. Of course there were other pickets besides me, but I did not know where the other boys were sent. A part of them went as far as the Orange Court House plank road, and then scattered in different directions, with only a few remaining for reserve from both companies, but it occurs to me that my post was the fartherest to the front. I think the other boys were posted mainly along the plank road.

I found the path barely wide enough to admit of the free movements of myself upon the horse. The hazel brush dragged my shoulders on either side, and occasionally I had to dodge a thorn, until I reached the eventful forks of the path. I found the rebel soldiers as stated by Captain Niven, apparently in consultation. I could easily see them as they stood out upon open ground, somewhat higher than that on which I stood, but I think I was completely hidden from them, being immediately surrounded by the dense wilderness of brush.

After remaining here for a half hour, more or less, I was startled by the reports of five or six shots fired directly in my rear and apparently on the path I had come. These shots, fired as they were, put a different phase on things, and I began to wonder if there were a chance for me to escape, hemmed in, as it were, on all sides, and no way to retreat except back as I came on this narrow path. My feelings were anything but pleasant. These thoughts all occurred to me like a flash, but I managed to stand it because I could not very well help it. Those rebels on my right stood there as though nothing had happened. This gave me a little encouragement to stand my ground, which proved to be all the worse further on. I listened with all the might I had for some return fire at the plank road, but in vain. The horse by this time had become demoralized, as it were. I could hardly keep him still, which added greatly to my embarrassment. But the rebels on the right stood there so firm, I concluded I would go back to the plank road and see if I could account for those shots fired. I knew this would ease the horse as well as myself, for I never like to stand still when in danger. On reaching the plank road, I was completely surprised at not finding any of our boys that were left as a reserve, and I was also equally surprised at not finding any rebels there, after discovering that our men were gone.

I stood there for some time, at least as long as I dared, not knowing but what those seven or eight rebels that I had left in my rear, might take a notion to ramble around as I was doing myself, and that I should meet them on this narrow path, when I turned back, if I could ever muster up courage enough to go back. Things would be a little mixed for a while any way. But I heard nothing. Everything seemed as silent as the grave, save the chirping of the little birds of the wild forest. Finally I resolved to return to the forks of the path, feeling that things might be all right. But here is where I made the mistake. I found the rebel soldiers, spoken of before, in nearly the same position as when I left; but almost as soon as I stopped, I saw two rebel infantrymen directly in my rear, and on the path that I had come on. They were coming toward me, and evidently had come from the plank road. They had not seen me yet, and apparently were noticing my horse's tracks and talking to themselves. This cut off my retreat.

Something had to be done immediately. I recognized this as quick as thought. At first they did not notice me, as I said before. This gave me the advantage for the time, and I fired three times in rapid succession, without halting them or saying a word, as that would have had a tendency to give them an equal advantage. The three shots seemed to be the limit of time for me, as they showed no signs of retreating or giving up. Between the second and last shots, the rebel in the lead fired his musket, the ball passing close to my left ear, but fortunately it did no damage, only caused a severe burning of that member, after I had sufficient time to appreciate it.

It was evident now, that I had to leave as best I could or surrender, and I concluded to try the former. I was afraid to shoot again, being a little afraid of my own marksmanship under the circumstances, the horse not standing still at any time during the melee, which I believe, and have thought a thousand times since, was the reason the rebel soldier did not hit me, as we were only a few feet apart. Those rebels on my right were now closely upon me, coming up the path, and consequently I had to move quickly, as they were mounted. Then, too, as if to give me warning that further efforts on my part to get away were useless, a volley of musketry echoed through the words suddenly, in the direction of the little cleared field, where I left the infantry in the morning, and it continued throughout the day. I now knew that I was completely cut off from our men, and that I was more than a mile in the rebel lines. But I seemed to be born of the spirit of that "while there is life there is hope."

I started down the left hand fork of the path as quick as possible. A few leaps of the horse took me out of reach and sight for the time, on account of the angling of the path, and the density of the timber. I dared not go far in this direction, however, and as soon as I reached a favorable point I made a break into the underbrush, and tried to make my way back to the army, parallel to the path leading back to the plank road that I had just left. But progress in this was slow, the most of the undergrowth being too large for the animal to go over successfully. By this time the woods were full of rebels and close around me. I thought they were slightly running over from the way they saluted me by yelling: " Halt, you yankee son of a b——," and some were not slow in shooting; while to say that I was scared is just putting it mildly. I had been in the army for some time, but the thought had not occurred to me yet how I would like to be a target, and so it was entirely original with me, and this is what made it worse.

As the rebels were advancing, I kept bearing to the right until I got lost, which by the way, did not take long, when there was nothing running at right angles to guide a fellow; even the setting sun was no guide to me in this case, as when that orb was disappearing over those southern hills it seemed to me as though it was in the south. The roar of battle now did not seem to lie in the same place, and the rebels were not advancing in the same direction. In running through the brush I had torn the saddlebags loose from the sides of the saddle, and had also torn the legs of my pants open to my knees. My arm was bleeding freely from a scratch by a thorn.

Notwithstanding my being lost, I now pressed towards the line of battle, thinking it my quickest and safest way out; for it appeared that the rebels had charged in from the west of our forces, which led me to think that the line of battle ran from northwest to southeast and that I was nearly at the extreme southern end of the lines. But this was imaginary. The fact is, I did not know where I was, only I had some idea that I was in Old Virginia. Then I lost my hat. I stopped a moment, not particularly for the hat, for it had no great value, but I had been running through the brush so long, and while moving I could not hear nor see to advantage, and it became necessary to stop and see if I needed to change my course. I did not see any rebels just then nor hear any bullets zipping past, and I slipped off the horse and got the hat. While picking it up, I heard one or two balls striking the limbs overhead. I remounted as soon as possible and was off. However, I soon crossed another path on a side hill, at nearly right angles. To the left and a short distance down the hill, there were several rebels drinking water from a spring. As I passed, one old fellow was just raising up, with the water still dripping from his unkempt and shaggy beard. He was actually the meanest looking man I ever saw, and he had a voice like a foghorn on a steamboat, only it was not quite so musical just then. He belched out, "There goes a yankee son of a b——!" and fired his gun. Then he yelled "Surrender!"

But I stuck to my text with a grace born of love, as the preachers sometimes say. Following this, the balance of them shot at me, but by this time I had passed their range and only one ball took effect, which luckily did no harm, only passing through the horse's mane just under my left hand as I held the reins.

Although surrounded by the rebels on all sides, it was rather unexpected for me to run on so many in a group, and so suddenly, and with the genuine rebel yell added, it nearly raised me from the saddle. It is just simply impossible for me to picture my feelings with a pen. The words "cold chills," so frequently used, is almost without a meaning in comparison. I had not gone far in this direction until I saw that it was no use. Then I began to get discouraged for the first time. I turned off to the right and a little to the rear.

I was now getting well nigh exhausted and the horse almost refused to go farther, but I spurred him up for one more effort at least. After travelling several rods, I came into another path on a slight elevation, and as I peeped over the hill, I saw that my doom was sealed so far as liberty was concerned. I rode out in the path, in plain sight, and dismounted so they would discover by degrees that I was a yankee. They were a squad of rebel cavalry watching the flank, and at first it appeared to me that they thought or regarded me as the advance of the yankees, as I noticed that they wavered a little, until the leader of the gang ordered me to surrender, which I did as he commanded without any hesitation, being glad to get a rest as it were, if I did have to submit to a rebel prison in the end, which it then seemed was my final destiny. But fate decided the case otherwise, as the reader will presently see.

They took everything marked "U. S." in my possession and a little that was not so marked. They ransacked the saddlebags and got all the extra ammunition I had stored away, which I ought to have been thoughtful enough to have thrown away before I surrendered, but I did not, and so the weapons were used to guard what they were intended to protect. They felt somewhat elated to think they had captured "a live yankee," as they called me to one another. They tantalized me some by telling me that they had a place for me down to Andersonville.

With me war with sword and gun was a thing of the past, and it was now a case of warring of ideas instead. They asked me various questions concerning the North and the Army of the Potomac. I answered all their inquiries, as near as possible, agreeable to myself; or in other words, in an evasive way, where an answer of that kind suited the case better, taking care not to let them know that such was the case. This made it appear discouraging to them and gave me great relief. I thought that if I could not beat them in one way, perhaps I could in another, in which I think I succeeded very admirably.

It was now nearly sundown and the battle was still raging and the bullets, rattling through the dry leaves now and then, could be heard distinctly from where we were.

Finally they decided to take me to where they had some more yankees, and then they said we would be shipped to Andersonville. We had not gone more than a half mile or so when we came to a cross path. Here they turned to the left and something attracted their attention, which caused them to stop and listen. There were three of them, one rode in front and two behind me. When we started, I asked permission to ride the horse. After parleying for some little time they finally consented reluctantly. While standing here, I noticed fresh horse tracks in the sand. This fired my drooping spirits, and I made up my mind that if those tracks were made by our cavalry they certainly could not be far away. But I said nothing; still, if those rebel guards had noticed me, I believe they would have seen a difference. In the meantime, the two horses behind me had got turned crossways of the path, with their heads to my right, and were eating the boughs. This was rather an unhandy position for them to shoot at me if I should happen to take French leave, which I was thinking very strongly of doing at the time, and I tightened the rein slightly, so my horse would step back and keep them from coming back into the path, and it all worked admirably without their noticing it in the least. While this was going on I saw some saber scabbards glistening through the brush, just a few rods ahead of us, for it was hardly dark yet, and I was satisfied that those were our men. There was a little clearing in the timber where they were, and I was not so sure but it was the little field I had left in the morning—that the army had advanced and had driven the rebels before them during the day.

The man in the lead now gave me orders to turn around. This gave me assurance that the rebel guards thought the same as I did in regard to the men ahead of us. As the rebel gave me orders to turn around, he commenced reining himself to the left, and so I did the same. However, as soon as I had got sufficiently out of his way, he turned altogether on the right hand side of me, and as he had started to turn first, it left no room for me to turn until he was out of the way. This left a reasonable excuse for me, just for the time being, and that was all I wanted of it. As soon as his horse's head was sufficiently turned to give me free access to the path, I put spurs to the horse, leaving them in a pile, so to speak, with two of them crosswise of the path and the other one faced about. The horse seemed to appreciate the situation as well as myself, and the way he left those rebels was a caution. My spur hung to the girth and when I undertook to let loose I came very near being thrown off, but I caught hold of the horse's mane and hung to it like a trooper. While thus engaged, I came up suddenly against a high fence. Not knowing but what the rebels were after me in my flight, I had no time to stay there on the horse and speculate on what might be the case, and I slid off on the ground and scampered into the woods before I looked in any direction. But when I saw the rebels were not following me I stopped, and I could just see a glimpse of them running from me. Then I looked the other way and saw some of our men in the opening inclosed by the fence. I now knew that I was safe, but I was afraid to go back to the path after the horse without some aid and so I gave a signal of distress, as it were, and I found that those men were one of our Generals of the army and his body-guard or escort, eight or ten private soldiers or orderlies, and he ordered his men to ride up and see what was the matter. He looked like our General Chapman of the Cavalry Corps, as he looked at me through his spectacles, but whether he was or not I never knew. I was too much overjoyed and nervous, generally speaking befuddled, to notice anything in particular.

Two of the orderlies rode up and guarded the premises while I led the horse through the fence. They were just leaving the field as I made my appearance, and as soon as I was up with them and the circumstances made known to the General, we moved on back to the army, which was not far distant. But, however, short as the distance was, we got on the wrong track and were fired upon by the rebels before we were aware that we were off of the road leading safely back. But we were not lost, and consequently in a few minutes we were on the right track again. We then crossed a little branch with running water and climbed the steep bank on the other side, where lay the dead and wounded of the day's struggle. Here we parted company, and the

General with his aides led off toward the log cabin spoken of on another page, while I kept straight ahead through a little neck of woods, where the road was still filled with wounded soldiers wending their way back to the hospital spoken of, which was carpeted only with the green grass and roofed with heaven's starry canopy.

It was now nearly dark, and firing along the line was still going on, but it was getting faint. On reaching the road that I had left in the morning, I found several of our boys, and they seemed overjoyed to see me once more and alive, for it had been reported by Alexander Carruthers, one of our company boys, who was posted along the plank road in the morning at the time the rebels made the charge, that he saw me fall from the horse at the commencement of the battle, but fortunately for me, he was mistaken. However, the report came very near being true several times during the day, without any of our men knowing it, for I believe I was not seen by our men after we parted at the plank road until I appeared upon the same at night. They all greeted me with a handshake and expressed surprise as I met them one by one, including Captain Niven and Captain Ford, who could hardly believe their own eyes as I stood before them. It was now about 9 o'clock, and the battle had almost died away, with only a stray shot now and then, and the soothing stillness began to brood over those Virginia hills. I was sore and weary, but managed to keep awake until I had seen all of the boys, then I wrapped up in my blanket and lay down upon the cold hard ground and watched the far off stars until the noise of the clattering of hoofs and the tramping of men were mingled with my dreams. In the morning we found that the rebels had withdrawn during the night. Then came the orders for us to retreat across the Rapidan, and finally back to our old quarters near Culpepper, together with the never-to-be-discouraged and never-to-be-forgotten Grand Old Army of the Potomac.

EARL W. SOPER.

BALBEC, Indiana, December 27th, 1888.

SKETCH OF COMPANY I, BY CAPTAIN W. H. HEALY.

Company I, like the rest of the companies, started out with two Captains and four Lieutenants—Captains, W. H. Healy and W. H. Webster; Lieutenants, Wm. Bartholomew, John Osborn, A. C. Hogoboom and Fred Scoville—but after being consolidated the officers were: Captain, Willard H. Healy from Oneida County; First Lieutenant, Wm. H. Webster of Monroe County; Second Lieutenant, A. G. Hogoboom of same county. It was some time before the company could decide on non-commissioned officers. The promise of the Colonel was that our extra Lieutenants should have some place in the other companies or on the staff; but of all these promises none were fulfilled. Our Colonel was true to his promise, but there being so many extra officers, he could not give all positions. After being in service for six months, Lieutenants Bartholomew and Scoville resigned and went into other regiments, after drilling with the regiment nearly all the winter of '61, and going through all the duties of camp life, also sharing all the honors of the regiment's mud moves.

The first duty of a soldier is to obey all orders. We expected every day to be sent home, as the government thought at the time there were too many soldiers, especially dismounted cavalry, we then having no arms but sabers. It was drill all day in saber exercise till we became perfect in that branch. Then came the old breech-loading Hall's carbine, that would kill more at the breech than at the other end. But all came in good time. We received orders to break camp and there were none but what were glad. We did not care where we went, only to get out of the mud. We then thought we could go to Richmond easy with our sabers, but afterwards found our mistake. We were ordered to pack tents, camp kettles and company property—but what a time we had! There was more in Company I than ten army teams could haul—chairs, bedsteads, stoves, and in fact furniture of all kinds. Where it had come from, as the boys had no money to buy and Company I had the name of taking nothing they could not reach, was more than the officers could tell. But as we must move, we took what we could, and left the rest for other poor soldiers.

Our first duty was picket duty on the Ohio and Chesapeake canal. Company I quarters were at Muddy Branch; the regiment's headquarters at Edward's Ferry. Well did Company I do their duty, as they picketed the most part of twenty miles. They fixed up old rafts, crossed the Potomac, and ten or fifteen men, with the Captain or Lieutenant, would go miles into Virginia, not thinking of any Johnnies. On one of these expeditions, the Captain with ten men visited a female seminary, where there were forty or fifty young ladies, all of them bitter secesh. But they got the men their suppers and pleasantly invited us to stay, but being so far from camp and in the enemy's country, we politely declined. We had a splendid supper. Bidding the ladies good-by, we started for camp, picking up on our way a pig or two, a few eggs, and poultry enough for all the company. We did not get back any too soon. Before we got across the river the rebels came in sight. That stopped foraging for a few days. But Company I was never contented, they must be roving. One little incident that happened at Muddy Branch will show how one soldier will treat another and share with him. We had to go to Edwards' Ferry for rations, which came on a canal-boat. Our commissary at that time was Lieutenant Bartholomew, and well he fed us. I think he must have reached a little. Among the rations at one time came a barrel of beer. Who ever heard of beer as a soldier's rations? All the same it came—from where, the Lieutenant claimed he did not know, when he reported to the Captain. It would not do to let the whole company know it, so it was concluded that it must go to the Captain's tent, as he never drank beer. There it would be safe, and the officers could get it without the privates knowing it. The Captain's tent was stretched over an old cellar where a log house had once stood. The ground was thrown up about two feet, the beer was brought in, a hole dug in the ground, the barrel put in so that there was only about eight or ten inches of earth on the outside, the barrel tapped and everything ready for the officers to have a good time. And they did, that evening, as long as the beer lasted. But it ran out long before it was expected, as the Captain had skipped out, gone down the line and got four or five of the boys to go with him, and tapped the barrel on the outside. While the officers were having a good time on the inside the boys were having a good time on the outside. But such is the life of a soldier. The officers were a little mad, but we think they never knew who gave them away. No harm now.

Our duty at Muddy Branch was light, but very tedious, as the weather was very disagreeable. If we had known it then, we would have been contented, as it was one of the easiest times we had while in service. We took time to visit the battlefields of Drainsville and Ball's Bluff and buried some of the dead that had been washed out of the trenches. Again came orders to get ready to move. When everything was packed, we had orders to mount, which we did, not horses, but a canal-boat, and sailed to Harper's Ferry, where we arrived in the spring of '62. The most forsaken town anyone ever saw. and such weather! We made ourselves as comfortable as we could the first night on the Maryland side of the Potomac river. The next day we moved on the soil of Old Virginia, the first time as a company and a regiment. The houses that belonged to the government were in good condition then, as the Johnnies had them for their quarters, and were not destroyed. Company I took possession of one or two of them, and had splendid quarters. Colonel Miles then being in command tried to get us to take muskets and act as infantry, but as the men had enlisted for cavalry they refused to take them. We expected to be attacked every day. Company I concluded to take muskets for emergency's sake. Did so, and were ordered on Maryland Heights where we marched, stacked our arms and began to enjoy ourselves the best way we could. At times you could not find half a dozen soldiers at headquarters of Company I, they were scattered all over the mountain. We stayed there until ordered down into Harper's Ferry again. Each soldier took a musket, but they had been stacked in front of our quarters for weeks, and rained full, which made them useless. Once more in Harper's Ferry, Colonel Miles ordered us to take muskets again and move out on the Harper's Ferry & Winchester railroad, but Company I, with the rest of the regiment, refused to move as infantry. Colonel Miles telegraphed to Washington that the regiment refused to obey orders. Company I did not move until nearly all of the company were sick. Poor rations had begun to tell. Colonel Miles called the Captain of Company I to headquarters, and, urging him to move, promised him the first station out of the Ferry, at Hallstown. The Captain would not consent without first consulting his officers and company. He returned to his quarters, called the company together, telling them how much better off we would be and how much easier it would be, and that we would have good rations. The company took a vote and left it to the officers whether they would go or not. The officers decided to go. Company I was the first company to march out of Harper's Ferry, but as we had refused to take muskets, we took the Hall's carbines, or what was left of them, for as we came from Muddy Branch, the boys broke up the most of them and threw them into the canal, but the next morning they were told that the guns were charged to them, and that they would have to pay for them. The most of the boys were armed again with the same kind of a gun. Where they came from the boys only knew. Some other company must have lost theirs. We marched to Hallstown, had beautiful quarters and healthy place, but the measles broke out in camp, and a great many had them and were very sick. By careful nursing all recovered. Whether it was the wine that cured them that came from the Chaplain is hard to tell. This is the way the wine was procured: The Captain went to Harper's Ferry, knowing that the Chaplain had received wine from the commissary, but the Chaplain told the Captain that one bottle and a half was all he had and he would give Company I the whole bottle, as the measles were so bad. He gave the Captain the bottle, and as he drew the case out from under his bunk the Captain saw that the case was full, or nearly so. He took the bottle and started for camp with his orderly, but was not satisfied. He waited until after dark, went back, told the orderly to dismount and hold the horses until he reconnoitered in the direction of the Chaplain's tent. He went to the back side of the tent, reached under, drew out the case with eight bottles, and returned to camp. The boys got their share and recovered from the measles. Whether the Chaplain ever knew who took his wine, history now will tell. This company was the out-picket for some time, until relieved by the Tenth Maine. The company then moved two miles above Charlestown, and its quarters were in a grist mill, and as there were eight millers in the company, the Captain being a miller himself, that accounts for the company being an honest company. They soon set the mill going, and the rest of the regiment having come from Harper's Ferry and on picket as far as Winchester, we made requisition on the farmers for grain, ground it, and supplied the community and regiment with flour and meal until we had to dig out.

May 28th, '62, Company I was at Harper's Ferry with no commanding officer but their own, as the regiment had been scattered by the way of Williamsport. The regiment was got together again, and sent to the Relay House, Maryland, to be mounted and equipped for the field. Then the fun began. We had been a wild company before. Now came the tug of war. Colonel B. F. Davis, a regular army officer, was appointed to the command of our regiment. "Old Grimes," as he was called by the boys of his old regiment, the Fifth United States Cavalry. If he were living to-day, he would be one of our star Generals. Strict in discipline but easy in all things to a good soldier, always at the head of the regiment, rough in language to his enemy until captured, then he was a friend to them. Our duty at the Relay House was light, but it was drill from morning until night. We had the finest horses furnished us. Some companies had black horses, and some bay. Company I was mounted on sorrels and as long as we were in camp they kept their color, but when once in service they began to be like Jacob's pigs, "Ringed, streaked an speckled." Some gay old times at the Relay House; never will the boys forget it until the last roll is called. Drilling and getting ready for the fall campaign. When all was ready we were ordered to Harper's Ferry once more. Arrived and went into the

Shenandoah Valley where we were so well known, scouting and having a brush now and then, until once more Stonewall Jackson was in the valley and after us again. Ordered into Harper's Ferry. We would slip out once in a while on a scouting expedition, but now under strict orders, as we had a Colonel who would take care of us now. It was on one of these scouting expeditions that the Captain of Company I captured five Johnnies alone, there being six, but one got away. It was this way. There was one mounted rebel that kept about shooting distance away from the company, calling us all kinds of names, telling us to come on. He was well mounted, but we could not get near enough to make our carbines tell. I asked permission to overtake him if possible. The Colonel gave consent. I called Orderly Buckingham to follow me. I struck off from the road, through a piece of woods to the right, thinking I could get in ahead of him, but when I came out to the road I was about ten rods in the rear. Then came the tug. We were both mounted on good horses. We commenced firing at each other. I got one shot through the left arm of the rebel, but could not catch him. We ran through a small piece of woods. There was a blacksmith shop close to the edge of the woods. In and around the door sat six Johnnies, with their guns leaning against the shop, but I was onto them so quick that they could not reach their guns in time, before I covered them. "Throw up your hands," was the first they heard. All did but one; he crawled through the fence and was out of sight in the cornfield. Up came the Sergeant, took their guns, covered them with his revolver, and I was off like the wind for the other Johnnie, but he was too far away. Soon a company of rebel cavalry came in sight, and then it was the Captain that had to get, which he did in good style, with Sergeant Buckingham with his five prisoners, all of them in good humor. All they could say was they would not have given up to one "yank," but they thought all the "yanks" at Harper's Ferry were there. We returned to Harper's Ferry without losing a man, only having a sharp skirmish with a company of rebel cavalry. Soon we were surrounded, and no way to get out. It was then that we began to appreciate what it was to have a good Colonel, as the future will show. The order from Stonewall Jackson was not to drop any shells into Harper's Ferry. He had an eye on the horses of the Eighth New York Cavalry. It was all the same; he did not get them. On Saturday evening, September 13th, a council of war was called, and permission asked by Colonel Davis of Colonel Miles to take the cavalry and cut its way out of Harper's Ferry. Permission was refused. On Sunday another council of officers was called, and Colonel Davis concluded if the officers would follow we would go out of the Ferry without asking Colonel Miles again. All agreeing, we were sent to have every company ready. It was raining slightly. When the bugle sounded the companies fell in nearly to a man. Company I was in the rear, and was ordered to keep all stragglers up, and well did they do their duty, and the regiment lost hardly a man. Away we went through the rebel lines. A Major of the Third Maryland Cavalry in advance, he having the countersign, we had no trouble in getting through, with but one small skirmish. Away we went, sometimes on the gallop, then smash into one another. We came to Williamsport pike just at daybreak, ran into General Longstreet's wagon train, cut the train in two and started them into Pennsylvania. Captain of Company I ordered to burn all wagons that broke down. Burned five. Private Abraham Louck was a soldier who was always in trouble, but always came out somewhere. When about half way up Maryland Heights Louck lost his horse over the bank. Louck got up almost killed, as he said, and wanted to know what to do. He was told to go to some farm house and stay until morning, and then give himself up to the rebels. There we left him. About one hour after that, as the whole regiment floundered through a mud hole, who should come up but Louck, the worst looking being you ever saw; covered all over with mud and water. "Hello, Louck, where did you come from?" "Can't lose me, Captain. I took one of the Pennsylvania Cavalry horses, and here I am." We came once more to a creek. Down goes Louck again, losing his horse once more, and washing the fellow quite clean, and nearly drowning him. We left him standing by the creek. On we went, and we gave him up as lost this time, but when we burned the wagons, who was blown out of the rear end of the wagon but Louck, his hair, whiskers and eyebrows burned off. We picked him up nearly dead, and as the Johnnies now came in sight, we had to get. We carried Louck to a farm house, and laid him on a bed, and as we supposed dead. Then we lit out. When we arrived at Green Castle and began to receive our rations from the farmers, who turned up again but poor Louck. He said: "Captain, I was killed once to-night by being thrown over the mountain, drowned twice, blown up and killed, but here I am, ready for all the rations I can get." Such was one of the many adventures coming out of Harper's Ferry. No time to rest. Away we go for Antietam to take a part in the battle. Stayed on the field until the battle was over. The next day were ordered to follow the Johnnies. A few more words, boys. Company I took its part with the regiment. The old officers are all alive, and the Captain is at present in Pennsylvania, entirely disabled, not having walked in three years; Lieutenant Webster is in Nebraska, Lieutenant Hogoboom in California, all enjoying small pensions on account of disability and wounds received in service.

CAPTAIN W. H. HEALY,
Blairsville, Pa.

EXPLOITS OF PETER BOYLE, COMPANY L.

COMRADE NORTON:—I see by the *National Tribune* that you are writing a history of the Eighth New York Cavalry and desire to get the names of pensioners and other members of the regiment. I was one of the original members of Company L. If you were with the regiment on the first or second of May, 1863, on the Rapidan river, you probably remember a soldier being shot on the fence by his carbine hammer touching the top rail. I am the chap. I had never missed a day's duty until that unfortunate day. Dr. Furguson dressed the wound. The boys told me afterwards they thought I could not live, so they placed pine boughs over me and then had to move off. The rebel battery across the river opened fire on that part of the woods just as if they were full of yankees. I got the full benefit of that fire alone, but was not hit. My brother was in the same company.

Four of the boys came back with a stretcher, and assisted Surgeon Vosburg, I believe, and carried me to a house on the west side of the railroad. There were left at the same house Lieutenant Phillips of the First Massachusetts Cavalry, shot through the neck; a First Rhode Island boy named Cableigh Rick and a South Carolina Cavalryman shot in the back. I saw the charge he was wounded and captured in that same day. A man named Butler was left to care for the Lieutenant and my brother to care for me.

In a few days after our cavalry left the rebels came and captured us. The rebels sent their surgeon to examine us. He said Phillips and I could not live to ride to Richmond. They paroled all hands. A day or two afterwards poor Phillips died. My brother and Butler buried him, and then struck a bee line for the Yankee Army, leaving Cableigh and me alone. We remained about two weeks. My wound was dressed every day by a colored woman. She also gave me all the information she could of where our army was. The old lady, who owned the plantation, had no male relatives and only one daughter to live with her. She tried to persuade me to stay with her. She said I would never be fit for a soldier again nor able to work, and if I would stay with her, I would have a good home, and oversee her plantation. Well, comrade, I did not stay. Duty to Uncle Sam, and a young lady in Monroe county forbade. I was then twenty-two. I was able to sit up, when one Saturday evening after dark, Cobleigh and I saw several camp-fires in the woods across the river. I heard the rebels unloading timber to build the railroad bridge that our boys had destroyed. We made up our minds to go, and go we did next morning. That march of twenty miles to the Rappahannock bridge on foot, I shall never forget. After we were captured, the rebels took everything we had, blankets, overcoats, ponchos, spurs, and among the rest my girl's picture, that I had carried so long in cold and storm. The Johnnies gave the picture to the old woman's daughter. When we were leaving, the young lady very kindly returned it to me, which I was glad to get. With my left hand in a sling and my right hand holding my broken left side together and the blood and matter running down into my boots, we took the railroad north. We got along very well by Mitchell Station, when we heard the command, "Halt!" from our rear. In looking around we saw a long lank Johnny charging down on us, mounted on a good horse, holding two navies, but with very poor clothes. We halted. "Who are yoh?" he said. "Union soldiers," I answered. "What are you doing here?" "Going to our lines," I replied. "What regiment do you belong to?" "The Eighth New York Cavalry," I replied. He said to Cobleigh: "What regiment do you belong to?" "The First Rhode Island Cavalry," Cobleigh replied. "G—— d—— the First Rhode Island Cavalry," he said. "They stole my sister's horses and took all her chickens and meat," at the same time he grasped one of his navies and covered my poor comrade with it. Cobleigh was not over twenty-one years old. Whether it was presence of mind or not I cannot say, but just as the "reb" was leveling his revolver at him, Cobleigh raised his right hand, and pointing to the "reb's" horse said, "Your saddle girth is loose." The "reb" looked down the side of his horse, at the same time his revolver dropped, and he did not raise it again. I can see those two men to this day just as plain as I saw them in May, '63, and I have every reason to believe that Cobleigh's remark about the saddle girth saved his life, and perhaps my own. He demanded our paroles. We showed them and he let us go. We reached Culpepper all right, and sat down on the depot steps to rest awhile. We were not there five minutes before we were surrounded by the whole population of the village. We got abuse from their tongues. A rebel officer came from a hotel across the road and took our part. He said we were soldiers the same as he was, and he would see that we were not injured by the crowd. He also said that he had escaped from our cavalry, and realized our position. We thanked him and started again, hoping we would get to the bridge without any more trouble. The old colored woman had told us that our men were at Rappahannock bridge. About half way from Culpepper to Brandy Station, we saw two horsemen coming towards us. As they got close, we saw that they were rebel cavalrymen. They did not take the trouble of halting us. When they got within five or six rods of us, they covered us with their carbines and we halted very suddenly without a word. They proved to be very nice fellows and gave us some tobacco and told us where we could get some buttermilk at an Irishman's house at Brandy Station. With our feet all blistered and my left boot nearly full of blood and matter, we reached the bridge at dark that evening. and were well taken care of. My brother, Thomas Boyle, who was left with me, arrived safe at Washington, joined the regiment some time that summer; was captured on the Wilson raid, in June, '64, starved in Andersonville all summer, was sent to Florence, South Carolina, in October and died there November 9th, 1864.

Three of my schoolmates of Company L were William Kelly, James Kelly, and Frank Daily. The Kelly boys got through safe ; Daily received a flesh wound in the valley near Fisher's Hill.

Yours in F. C. & L.,
PETER BOYLE.

CANANDAIGUA, N. Y., November 17th, 1888.

HENRY NORTON—*My Dear Comrade:*—You say you would like me to write some reminiscences of the war in which the Eighth New York Cavalry took an active part. I will state a few facts that I have never seen in history, namely, that I and comrade Wm. Rollinson captured two prisoners just after daylight on the first day of the battle of Gettysburg, while on picket southwest from Gettysburg on a cross road where a little creek ran south on the east side of the road. We had just relieved two men who had been on the same post. Just as the men started from the post, and while letting their horses drink at the creek, two shots were fired. The two men galloped away. I turned my horse up the west road and in the field to the right stood two "rebs" in the act of loading their muskets. I ordered them to surrender, which they did. I marched them down the road and just as we got down to where Rollinson was, our bugler, Dennis Curren, called us in to join our company. We took our prisoners and joined the company. In the excitement I do not know who took charge of the prisoners, but I do know that we went into the fight. Just one month after that, when we charged that battery between Brandy

Station and Culpepper Court House, on the first day of August, 1863, after I was wounded in my left arm at the shoulder, I captured a South Carolina cavalryman. He did not know that I was wounded until afterwards. When he found out that I was wounded, he said if he had known it he would not have surrendered to me. He said it was "a d——n yankee trick anyway." It is admitted that the Eighth New York Cavalry fired the first shot on the Union side at Gettysburg, and I believe I captured the first prisoner.

Yours truly in F. C. & L.,
ALFRED W. DAVIES,
Company F, Eighth New York Cavalry.

WALTHAM, Iowa, January 5th, 1889.

HENRY NORTON—*Dear Sir and Comrade:*—Being a subscriber to the *National Tribune* (that great soldier's friend) I saw your request for comrades to write to you. As to any great thing that I did personally I have nothing to boast of, but this much I do feel proud of, that I was a member of the old Eighth Cavalry, whose record as a cavalry regiment is second to none, and that I always tried to do my duty. None can say that I ever shrank from a place of danger and I always kept my place under all circumstances.

I enlisted September 27th, 1861, at Seneca Falls, N. Y., in Company G, as private, was made a Corporal before we left Camp Hill House, and then Duty Sergeant at Harper's Ferry in 1862, promoted to First Sergeant July 1st, 1864, and when we were reorganized was transferred to Company C as First Sergeant and was commissioned as Second Lieutenant with rank, from April 13th, 1865. Participated in all the engagements with the regiment until mustered out. Was not wounded, but as to close calls, I had several balls through my clothes, and one came very close, passing between the upper-leather and the sole of my boot, making my leg lame for some days; thus escaping the balls. But not so with disease. I contracted diseases on our campaign in the valley, for which I am now drawing a pension of ten dollars per month from September 8th, 1886, and was given arrears of four dollars per month from date of discharge to the above date, discharge dated June 27th, 1865.

This is all I think of now that would be of interest to you as history. Comrade, how well I would like to see you and the old boys that passed through and were tried by fire in that dreadful war.

Yours truly in F. C. and L.,
MILTON REYNOLDS,
Second Lieutenant Company C.

ARKONA, Lambton Co., Canada, Jan. 4th, 1889.

NOTES.

The survivors of the Eighth New York Cavalry will remember Charles G. Hampton, of Company H. He enlisted September 28th, 1861, was taken prisoner, at the battle of Winchester, May 25th, 1862, confined in rebel prison about four months, and was then exchanged and returned to the regiment. He was promoted to Corporal, February 14th, 1863; to Sergeant, August 19th; Second Lieutenant, October 5th, 1863; First Lieutenant and transferred to the Fifteenth New York Cavalry. He was wounded and taken prisoner on the 20th of February, 1864, soon after he took command in his new regiment, went through all the horrors of a rebel prison for thirteen months more; was promoted to Captain February 13th, 1865, and discharged May 15th, 1865.

The survivors of the Eighth New York Cavalry will remember John E. Ayer, of Company E. He now resides at Washington, D. C., and is employed by the government in the Treasury Department. He was wounded at Funkstown, Maryland, July 9th, 1863, and suffered the loss of his left foot, and was discharged October 5th, 1863, on account of wound at Frederick, Maryland.

Enos Guile, Walter B. Norton and Henry Lagard Norton, of Company H, bore charmed lives. They enlisted in 1861, when the regiment was first organized; they were in almost every engagement in which the regiment participated; they had men killed and wounded on both sides of them; they re-enlisted in the spring of '64 and followed the regiment through to the end of the war, and came home without a scratch. Many of the regiment went through and came out the same way.

The surviving comrades will remember William Ford of Company D. He is now living in Preston, England. He says that he is well pleased that one of the boys of the Eighth New York Cavalry has got up enough courage to write up the history of the regiment. He was taken prisoner at the battle of Culpepper, 1863, and had a taste of rebel prison for a short time.

Comrade Earl W. Soper wishes to inform all comrades that he has been appointed Notary, and has the authority to obtain pensions for comrades. Any communications from comrades will be highly appreciated and promptly attended to. Address, Balbec, Jay County, Ind.

ORIGINAL ROSTER OF THE REGIMENT.

FIELD AND STAFF OFFICERS.

Samuel J. Crooks...Colonel
Charles R. Babbitt...Lieutenant Colonel
William L. Markell..Major
William H. Benjamin...Major
James Chapman..Surgeon
Winfield S. Fuller..Assistant Surgeon
Albert L. Ford..Adjutant
Frederick H. Barry..Quartermaster
Frederick W. Clemons..Battalion Adjutant
Theodore B. Hamilton.....................................Battalion Quartermaster
Frederick Scoville...Battalion Adjutant
William H. Webster...Battalion Quartermaster
William Ross..Brevet Sergeant

COMPANY A.

Edmond M. Pope............Captain | Alfred Leggett......First Lieutenant
Alfred E. Miller...Second Lieutenant.

Andrew T. Leggett	Marcenus H. Cole	Charles F. Merrick
Northrop Needham	Luther F. Corbin	Alexander Mitchell
Peter Brewer	Andrew J. Cook	John McCormac
Almond P. Strowger	Lawrence Cullen	James Nichil
Edward P. Follett	George W. Clark	John O. Neil
Charles Harrison	Albert Cooper	Wm. B. Olmsted
William H. Norton	Horace W. Daggett	Horace Peet
H. Orson Pope	Jacob DeKnbber	George Reeder
William Hector	Peter J. DeMaille	George Ritz
Edwin A. Slocum	Chester J. Desmond	George Reas
Jerome M. Doubleday	Robert B. Dikeman	Wm. Smith
William C. Lathrop	Abraham Downing	Nelson Smith
Frank A. Thompson	Samuel H. Duell	Jacob Schillinger
James Brown	Edward W. Dimock	John Schulick
George Oscar Hale	Edward Easling	Charles Stevens
Edward M. Voorhees	Albert H. Edson	John Schroeder
William H. Steigelmaier	John Futherer	Isaac Scout
Wm. H. Anderson	Farrel Gallagher	John Shehan
George W. Clark	John Gallagher	James W. Tailor
Harmon Burroughs	Andrew J. Gouldswardt	Jay Van Alstine
Horace A. Ackley	Peter Hallings	John R. Vontana
Harvey H. Brown	John Hendricks	Charles Viergever
Michael Blake	Bart Hallings	Matthew Vontana
Edward Bushler	Wm. Hill	John Van Horn
Samuel Burnett	Gotlieb Konath	August Wagner
George L. Blauvelt	John Lassen	Squire Worden
Charles M. Booth	Henry Light	Oliver Weyburn
Addison Clark	John A. Miller	

COMPANY B.

Caleb Moore..................Captain | Henry J. Cutler......First Lieutenant
John A. Broadhead......Second Lieutenant.

James Bliss...............	John Canfield............	Dudley M. Lewis.........
Joseph O. McClosky.....	John Calaghan...........	Henry Larey.............
John H. Dusenberry....	George W. Clickner.....	Willshire Lockwood.....
Charles S. Curtis........	Chas. W. Carpenter.....	Orin Larkin.............
Martin Hogan............	Addison Chamberlin....	John Ladding............
Samuel Churchill........	Josiah B. Davis..........	Alex. McMillin..........
William H. Cline........	Joseph Dani.............	James P. Madison.......
Martin I. Taylor........	Joseph Davis............	Patrick J. McEvoy......
Jacob Chamberlain.....	Charles Dancy...........	John McGrath...........
John J. Brown...........	Wm. Dickenson..........	Geo. W. McKinzie.......
Franklin L. Robbins....	Isaac H. Edwards.......	Albert Paxon............
Jeremiah Hickman......	Joseph W. Flint.........	Henry Pomeroy.........
Robert Tafft.............	Jacob Friend.............	Robt. S. Powers.........
Alonzo G. Robb.........	Granville M. Gilbert....	Valentine Pike..........
Edwin G. Smith.........	Hugh Gateus............	Fred'k Peck ....
Benj. W. Middaugh.....	John H. Hounsom.......	Jonas B. Rothrick.......
Thomas H. Taylor......	Erastus Hanchett.......	Wm. H. H. Robinson....
Samuel McAnn..........	William Hobden.........	David Roach.............
Horatio W. Smith.......	Albert S. Hibbard.......	Wm. Raker..............
Minard Averill..........	James Hallighan........	John Shaeffer...........
John Agon..............	Peter Hoffmen..........	Casper Shaeffer.........
Henry Averill...........	Wm. Hobbs..............	Henry Smith............
George T. Ashdown.....	Orrin Jump..............	Wm. Slade..............
Horace A. Baker........	Wm. Jennings...........	Orson Treadwell........
Wm. H. Barnum.........	Rich M. Jones...........	Chas. Van Klin..........
Lawrence Behl..........	Thomas Johnson........	Walter Woodham.......
Myron A. Bell...........	Horace Keith............	Chester Weaver.........
Stewart H. Bell.........	John Kline...............	Alfred Williams.........
Christopher Conners....	Joseph Kurfurst.........	John Weaver............
Abel E. Crippen.........	Matthew King...........	Joel Wood..............
Daniel Culbert..........	Robert Lyday...........	Samuel Welkley........

COMPANY C.

John W. Dickerson............Captain | John Brown.........First Lieutenant
Fred W. Clemens..Second Lieutenant.

Eli H. Allen..............	Wm. M. Fisk............	James Pearce...........
Edward Ades............	George W. Failing.......	Charles W. Roberts.....
Philip Assimus..........	Wm. Fillmore............	Jackson Robinson.......
Wm. J. Baily............	Michael Foley...........	Wm. H. Rogers.........
George Brown...........	John B. Graves..........	Marcus D. Reynolds....
Albert Butts.............	John Heinburk..........	John W. Randall........
Elisha S. Chapman.....	Darwin Harrington.....	Edwin K. Robinson.....
Wm. Chapman..........	Eugene V. Harrington..	Jas. M. Robinson.......
Benj. M. Carl............	Otis Humphrey..........	George Reynolds.......
Malcom H. Carl.........	George Hurgate.........	Wm. P. Reeves.........
John Corwin............	John C. Hopkins........	John N. Reeves.........
George A. Clark........	Gideon P. Irish..........	James E. Reeves.......
Wm. Cunningham.......	Francis A. Ireland.......	Judson E. Rice.........
George A. Culver.......	Wm. Jenkins............	George H. Randall.....
Charles H. Cleveland...	Jacob Larisher..........	Joseph C. Reeves......
Elijah Dumalt...........	John Lund..............	James Rustin...........
Walter H. Douglass....	Wm. Ladue.............	Robert Stewart........
Archibald Dickenson...	Wm. Mills...............	Robert N. Shipey......
Horace Dearborn.......	David Myers............	Loren Sherwood.......
Lyman H. Essex........	George H. Matthews...	Jacob Stutler..........
Eccuert G. Everett.....	John Murray............	Sidney Stickles........
Alfred Eastley..........	Wm. H. Moore..........	Wm. J. Shavom........
Devalencourt Fish.....	Harvey Olmstead.......	Charles Stace..........
Milton M. Failing.......	Edward O'Neil..........	Edgar G. Trask........

EIGHTH NEW YORK CAVALRY. 153

Wm. H. Taylor.............
George S. Town..........
Rich S. Taylor............
Samuel P. Thompson....
Fred S. Ulrich.............

John H. Ulrich............
Edwin VanWormer......
Abram VanWormer......
Daniel D. Willis,..........
Philip Weaver............

Jacob Wheat..............
Joseph Zeigler............
Merrill D. Zeymor.......

COMPANY D.

Wm. Frisbie.................Captain | Ezra Z. Peck........First Lieutenant
Albert L. Ford....Second Lieutenant.

Christian Aichinger.....
Charles Adsit............
Charles E. Banta........
Albert E. Brooks.........
Henry C. Bridger........
Wallace Blackman.......
Jacob Beck................
Bradford M. Leeman....
Henry Bush...............
Christopher Bannister..
Thaddeus Bannister.
Samuel H. Combs........
James R. Colburn.......
John S. Converse........
Cuyler Coats..............
Charles H. Church......
John W. Case.............
Joseph Collins............
Patrick Cunningham....
Wm. L. Carncross........
John Durham.............
John Dennis...............
Charles Drake............
John Dunker
Benjamin Edwards......
Rensselaer Gardner.....

Wm. German.............
Fred Gaylord.............
John H. Gill...............
James L. Hicks..........
Charles Haskins.........
David Hollenbeck........
George M. Hunt..........
Robert S. Hawks.........
John Ham..................
David Knight.............
John Kane.................
Wm. Lovejoy..............
Jeremiah Millard........
Albert Millard............
John E. Miller............
Chas. McGrain...........
Henry Marsh..............
John McIntyre...........
Nathan Masters..........
George E. Mack.........
Patrick O'Brien..........
Maurice O'Donnald.....
James W. Playford......
Stephen Playford........
Charles L. Patterson....
Reuben Pierson..........

Linus Parsons............
Charles W. Pierson......
Charles Pease............
Alfred B. Ruperts........
George S. Readfield.....
William Richards........
Eli Rogers..................
Edson Smith...............
Thos. G Secor............
David Smith...............
John Sahlman.............
Cornelius Spoor..........
Chas. H. Spoor............
Chas. N. Sears............
Wm. Sholes................
Brainard Spoor...........
Wm. H. Story.............
Wm. H. Thompson......
Robert H. Tripp..........
Frank L. Thompson.....
Robert VanDusen........
John A. Wood.............
John Wood..................
Daniel Wood...............
Albert Wetmore..........

COMPANY E.

Benjamin F. Foot.............Captain | Alpha Whiton........First Lieutenant
Theodore B. Hamilton..Second Lieutenant.

George R. Achilles......
John Austey...............
John E. Ayer...............
Harrison Alexander.....
Carlos V. Beecher.......
Horace Bacon,.............
Chester F. Barry........
Lewis Burch...............
Daniel S. Brown.........
Alex H. Braddock........
Albert M. Bristol.......
John C. Brown............
Philo Burch................
Addison Barton..........
Alex Barton................
Henry Bickford..........
Almond Brightman......
Amos A. Castle...........
Daniel Corner.............
John Cline..................
James Congdon..........
Henry K. Christman....

Wm. Cassidy..............
Wm. Davis..................
Newton Fisk..............
Charles A. Fox...........
Wm. T. Fearby..........
James N. Garrett........
Henry Griffiths..........
Thomas Hartley.........
David Hinman............
Willis S. Hinman........
Augustus Hause.........
Oscar Jones...............
James Johnson...........
Lewis Kane................
Peter Kelly................
George Long..............
Henry H. Lathrop.......
James H. Marion........
Thos. H. Murphy.......
James O'Neil.............
Harrison D. Odiskirk...
Chester D. Owens......

George Rifenbonk.......
Bailey Roberts............
James K. Robson........
Thomas Richardson....
Wm. G. Richardson.....
Nelson A. Rude..........
Charles Ross..............
Robert Ramshaw........
George Sheriff............
George Skeel..............
Carlos F. Smith..........
Albin Stearns.............
Orrin Smith................
Wheaton R. Southworth
Thomas Strouse..........
John S. Schaller.........
Christian Snyder........
James P. Thorn..........
James N. Tucker........
Elijah Watton.............
Franklin Wright.........
Charles Ware.............

EIGHTH NEW YORK CAVALRY.

Jerome Wright..........
David Walsh.............
Allen A. Willson.........
Robert H. Watkins......

James Watterson........
Henry Westerman.......
Samuel C. Ward.........
Albertus Wilcox.........

Bradley S. Webster......
Henry Winegardner....
Charles Wallace.........
John Zimmerman.......

COMPANY F.

Fennimore T. Gallett.........Captain | Thomas Bell.........First Lieutenant
Wm. M. Brtstol...Second Lieutenant.

George Acker............
George W. Armstrong...
Wesley M. Bonnett......
George W. Bowen.......
Oliver J. Barry...........
Charles H. Barry........
Albert Barnes............
Edward Babcock........
Charles Bahn............
Chandler Britton........
George P. Beam..........
Dennis Curran..........
George P. Curtis.........
James Campbell.........
Lindorf H. Carll.........
Wm. H. Derby...........
Walter Doty..............
John Davis...............
Daniel Doyle.............
Daniel Donovan.........
Wm. Davies..............
Joseph Elsome..........

Thomas Flannagan......
Robert Galusha..........
Pat Griffin................
Charles A. Green........
Daniel E. Haskell........
Wm. Howell..............
Hiram Jerome...........
Charles Jerome..........
Joseph P. Johnson......
John Kirby...............
Lewis F. Kellogg........
George W. Morris......
VanRensselaer McComber...
James Moran............
Thomas E. Mills.........
Myron Owens...........
John W. Piatt............
Charles A. Phillips......
Lysander Robbins......
Charles Rosch ....
Joseph Randall.........

Wm. H. Smith...........
James E. Smith..........
Manley A. Safford......
Robert A. Safford.......
David Swarthout.......
Henry Snyder...........
Eben F. Snyder..........
James P. Swain.........
Calvin Smith.............
Daniel W. Sandford.....
John H. Shutt............
James H. Swarthout,...
Patrick Smith............
John H. Tower..........
Russell W. Tibbetts......
James B. Treat..........
DeWitt C. Wilcox........
Herbert W. Webster.....
Joseph Wermer.........
Frank E. Willett.........
Augustus Manchester...

COMPANY G.

Benjamin F. Sisson...........Captain | Frank O. Chamberlin... .First Lieut.
Samuel E. Sturdevant...Second Lieutenant.

Elias V. Rugar............
Eli G. Coe.................
Hartwell B. Compson...
Wm. H. H. Page.........
Milton Reynolds.........
Bainbridge Douglas.....
Oscar J. Bassett..........
Henry A. Bull............
E. Delafield Dwelle......
George Shaffer...........
DeForest Spencer........
Wm. A. Whitehead......
Wm. E. Hart..............
Walter Hoag..............
Levi Walker..............
Wm. Vutterville..........
Ebenezer Washburn....
Levi C. Page..............
Charles B. Andrus.......
Robert Bailey.............
Charles Burtch...........
Henry T. Barnes.........
Daniel Burbank..........
John N. Budlong........
Wm. Bellman............
Warren O. Card.........
Edward Costelle.........

John W Davis............
Wm. DeScham..........
Frederick Duch..........
Samuel Englor..........
Nelson E. Evans.........
Lucius I. Fuller...........
Robert Furguson........
Christian Flukefeller...
Stephen B. Griggs.......
George Hopkins.........
Daniel Hull...............
Avary Ingraham.........
Daniel King...............
Andrew J. King..........
Chester A. King..........
Miles Knickerbocker....
Henry D. Lewis..........
Wm. A. Long............
Aaron Lamoreaux......
Joseph E. Leigh.........
George Livingston......
Wm. Linkenberg........
James McHosker.......
Amandus Miller.........
Albert S. Mitchell........
Charles Minor............
Harvey A. Metcalf.......

Isaac Mapes..............
George W. Molatt......
Asher L. Nichols........
Wm. E. Pine..............
Caleb Pierce..............
John Pruyn...............
Thomas S. Powers......
Frederick Prouty ....
George R. Redman.....
John Snyder..............
Cyrus Snyder............
Edwin A. Scott..........
John F. Sloat.............
Theodore Stearns.......
Charles Stearns.........
Leonard Stewart.......
Myron Sloat..............
Jacob Simmedley.......
Horton Travis............
Richard Taylor..........
Isaac Tooksberry.......
Francis Tibbles..........
I. Newton Wilcoxen.....
Arnold Walbridge......
Thomas Waller..........
Charles H. Warren......

EIGHTH NEW YORK CAVALRY. 155

COMPANY H.

George H. Barry............Captain | Alfred Kinney........First Lieutenant
Daniel E. Sackett........Second Lieutenant.

Wm. D. Adams............	Michael Downey.........	Henry Norton...........
Square Bowers............	Charles D. Follett........	Legard Norton...........
Hid Brockway............	George Foot............	Walter B. Norton........
Wm. W. Burnett..........	Wm. Grunwell...........	Peter Neshon...........
John Burgont............	John Clinch............	Wm. F. Parkhurst.......
Michael Burnes...........	Wm. Guile..............	Albert Peck............
Stephen H. Barnes.......	Enos Guile..............	Edwin B. Paul..........
Nelson R. Brown.........	Charles D. Geer.........	Darwin Pierce..........
George W. Brooks........	Charles Graves..........	Frederick Pilgrim.......
Gilbert Brown............	Dwight Hamilton.......	George H. Ross.........
Edmund Beasley.........	Charles G. Hampton....	Morton M. Reed........
Philander Bowdish.......	Marganzie Hopkins.....	George Rhodes.........
Edward Bensing.........	Wm. Howard...........	Charles Rapp..........
Alonzo Brockway,.......	Gilbert Harvey..........	David Shippey, Jr......
Sidney M. Briggs........	Wm. C. Kerwin.........	Albert Scott...........
Walter Cook.............	Daniel Kehoe...........	Stephen D. Scott.......
Christopher Caine.......	John Kehoe.............	Wm. Sage..............
John Copeland...........	Henry Lovejoy..........	Charles Spencer........
Henry C. Carr...........	Riley Lowe.............	George C. Shepard.....
Howard L. Chase........	Teunis Lowe...........	Wm. Stutcill...........
Benjamin Casper........	Israel Lynch............	Augustus Stubz........
Wm. H. Cotton..........	Daniel D. Main.........	Adin B. Taylor.........
Benjamin Curtis.........	Edward A. Miner.......	Jacob VanAlstine.......
Milo Church.............	Peter Maynor...........	J. B. Vanderhoof.......
John L. Church..........	Charles McFarland.....	Thomas P. Whiteing....
Andrew M. Dickenson...	John McFarland........	George Winzer.........
Edward Day.............	Daniel Nellis...........	Louis Zimmerht........

COMPANY I.

W. H. Healy................Captain | Wm. H. Webster......First Lieutenan
F. Scoville........Second Lieutenant.

Fayette Allen............	Eugene Ferry...........	Thomas Mercer.........
Henry Andrews..........	Zima M. Fuller.........	John M. McCarthy......
Joseph S. Atwood........	W. H. Foot............	Charles Morgan........
Eli Bradish..............	James Griffith..........	Levi Munger...........
A. S. Babcock...........	Clark A. Gates..........	John Moss.............
Samuel Butter..........	Henry Goodfellow......	John Osband..........
John A. Binlison.........	Orlen Gould............	Frank Pesso...........
Albert Buckingham.....	Stephen Haskins........	Jacob Perrin..........
Wm. Bronson...........	Charles Hammond.....	Smith Pratt...........
David Covil.............	Conrad Hallaner.......	Wayne I. Peck.........
Charles O. Clark,.......	Henry Heith...........	Leroy Pratt...........
John Coil...............	Nelson Herrick.........	Austin B. Pixley.......
George W. Cathrill......	Smith Hollister.........	Sylvester Shaffer.......
Patrick Callaghan.......	Patrick Hayes..........	Elam Scribner.........
Albert Camp............	Lewis Hunt............	George Stebbins.......
Frank Carrol............	Horace Harrington.....	Henry Stedman.......
Charles Carrol..........	Thomas Harly..........	Myron Strange........
Philander Cooper.......	Thomas Jones..........	Oliver Sutton.........
Wm. H. Dickey.........	Henry Jeffrey..........	George Schlegel.......
David Dusenbury.......	John Kirkwood.........	John Schlegel.........
R. E. Dillingham.......	John Kallacer..........	Adolph Segrist........
Wm. Donahue..........	Thomas Kelly..........	Robert Stebbins.......
Charles D. Davis.......	David Lawrence........	Wm. P. Sergent.......
Wm. W. Delong........	Abraham Louck........	James Sykes..........
Francis Denman........	Richard Murphy.......	James H. Seals........
Emery Eaton...........	Joseph Murphy........	Alpha Utley..........
Henry Fielding.........	Henry Moor............	Nathan Uphegrove.....

156 EIGHTH NEW YORK CAVALRY.

Melvin Vanloan..........	John Wall...............	Square Wiser............
Robert VanVechten.....	John Weaver............	Charles Williams.......
Henry Walker...........	Joel C. White...........	Jacob Witmore..........
Roderick White..........	Wm. Wiley...............	Wm. Wesley.............

COMPANY K.

John Weeland................Captain | John Shoen..........First Lieutenant
George Fochner......Second Lieutenant.

Josef Appllediney........	George Guenster........	Frederick Ross..........
Martin Auberf............	Anton Gutnacht.........	James R. Ried...........
Wm. Booner..............	Charles Glevee..........	Charles Raynolds........
Michael Brandigan......	Max Grossman..........	Josef Schmid............
Francis Breitenbach....	Wm. Greenwell..........	Philip Stoll..............
George Balg..............	Myron Gibbs.............	Emanuel Seigs...........
Charles Bek..............	Owodstean Haller.......	John Stumpf............
John Betsher.............	James Holmes...........	Christian Sellbach......
Frederick Bachman.....	Reuben Harwey.........	Peter Shaeble...........
Philip Bek................	Conrad Kilian...........	Thomas Steikel.........
Josef Bauer...............	Frederick Kuhn.........	Julius Sans..............
Louis Bauer...............	Constantin Krieg........	Adam Staeech...........
Zacharias Baumgarten..	Martin Kregser..........	Theodore Shweizer......
Nathan Bowen............	Jacob Kraemer..........	John Sutter.............
Lorenzo Brown............	Jacob Lee................	John Silliman...........
James Bennett............	John Lerch..............	Ezra Soles...............
Josef Beadle..............	Adam Lingh.............	Anton Thalheimer......
Josef Brownger...........	Theodore Luther........	Charles Tomba..........
John Cook.................	Christian Maelander....	Theodore Tyler..........
Samuel Church...........	Jacob Maier.............	Reinhard Volger........
Wm. Crowell..............	Christian Merkel........	George Vittey...........
Daniel Campbell.........	Frederick Merton.......	James Van Sikler.......
Leonard Conklin........	George Myers............	Henry Walter...........
Nicholas Camp...........	John McGuire...........	Adam Westenfelder.....
George Camp.............	Edwin Munger..........	Charles Wolf............
Henry A. Colborn.......	George Marks...........	Frederick Wheeler......
Gotthold Diehl...........	Haram Munk............	George Witney..........
Edwin W. Dunook.......	Augustus Nicholas......	Adolph Wittenberg.....
Thomas Dewer...........	Michael Quinn...........	Nicholas Wiles..........
John Doran...............	Wm. Pinchin............	George Wilson..........
Edam Dowel..............	John Reomek............	Franklin White.........
Thomas Dellon...........	Mosig Rohrbach.........	Charles Warren........
Henry Dunk..............	John Riedel..............	Wm. Yates..............
Enik Fresh................	Leonhard Ross...........	August Zshorsh........
Eleazer Fordham........	Charles Reinhard.......	

COMPANY L.

James W. Hooker..............Captain | Horace B. Hooker...First Lieutenant
James McNair........Second Lieutenant.

Charles T. Van Dusen...	Wm. H. Osborn.........	Elijah Burch............
Noah Sellick..............	Lucas B. Brewster......	H. B. Baldwin..........
Wm. Hunt................	Charles H. Brewster....	John Jay Bloss.........
Alfred G. Perkins.......	Fred S. Bailey...........	Thos. Boyle.............
Edward A. Britton......	Peter Boyle..............	Allen Benedict..........
Albert Huntington......	Wm. W. Bartlett........	Alanson Britton........
Thomas S. Farr..........	James Bailey............	David Cramner.........
Andrew Kirder...........	Andrew J. Bastion.....	Wm. Cain...............
George A. Griswold.....	John H. Burns..........	Patrick Cusack.........
H. H. Fairbanks.........	John Baty...............	John Curragher........
Enos McDowall...........	Enos Boardman........	Henry D. Clark........
Charles A. Goheen......	Seneca Bragg............	Frank Dailey...........
Stanton E. Frisbee......	James H. Bailey........	Michael Doyle..........
Nicholas McAvoy........	Thomas J. Brown......	John E. Doty...........

EIGHTH NEW YORK CAVALRY. 157

John DeGraff............
David H. Francis........
John Gallagher..........
Chas. Glein.............
John Gamrod.............
Wm. Hughes..............
Joseph Hall.............
D. C. Hammond...........
Nicholas Hay............
Andrew Hauser...........
Daniel Hull.............
Jehial Johnson..........
Jas. F. Kimpson.........
James Kelley............
Wm. Kelley..............
Horace Lillie...........
Oscar E. Loomis.........
Wm. Logan...............
Chas. H. Little.........
Edward Mehan............

Dan Morrisey............
Michael McPhillips......
Robt. M. Moore..........
Henry Monroe............
James Mosher............
Wm. McCrone.............
George Niner............
Henry Predmore..........
Patrick Quinn...........
L. B. Quagle............
Wm. O. Raymond..........
Joseph Raisinger........
James Ryan..............
George Rice.............
Joseph Ringelsprager....
Jacob Rufer.............
G. W. Reynolds..........
Andrew Robinson.........
John M. Rache...........
Nathan Scribner.........

Jason C. Spear..........
Charles Stevens.........
Horace C. Sloan.........
Sebastian Smith.........
Festus U. Spriggs.......
Dan G. Summers..........
H. H. Tillittson........
John C. Van Ness........
Moris Van Holst.........
R. Q. Williston.........
Herman Wimple...........
Newton Wing.............
Silas White.............
Edward W. Williams......
Jacob Wesley............
Wm. Werren..............
Wm. H. Whitstone........
John J. Wimple..........

COMPANY M.

Vincent M. Smith.............Captain | Henry C. Frost......First Lieutenant
            B. Chedelle Erner........Second Lieutenant.

Lewis V. Griffin........
Jervis W. Newton........
Benjamin F. Chappell....
George Duget............
Robert Niver............
Allen M. Beebe..........
Lewis Gray..............
Charles Mills, Jr.......
Andrew J. Whitney.......
Thomas Sweeney, Jr......
Charles Cagelm..........
Milton Culver...........
Monroe M. Copp..........
Walter V. Banning.......
John C. VanGilsen.......
Albert Stiles...........
Robert Abel.............
Jacob C. Andrews........
David Bruce.............
Mark Belson.............
James B. Bruce..........
Henry T. Baker..........
John Bradford...........
David Clark.............
Richard Clinton.........
Alex M. Caruthers.......
Daniel Collins..........
Theo. H. Cagean.........
John Clascow............
Edward Case.............
Wilson Caruthers........
Simon DeRidder..........
Adam Daylor.............
Joseph Duffner..........

James A. Dunham.........
Daniel Dismore..........
Fred K. Dodge...........
Abram DeClark...........
Sylvester Edwards.......
Isaac Erniss............
Wm. Fulford.............
Libbens Gier............
George W. Giles.........
Wm. Gleason.............
John Grunwell...........
Edward Gott.............
Jacob Guenther..........
George Grass............
Wm. H. Howland..........
Geo. Hosmer.............
Addison G. Hiscock......
Robert Haslip...........
Volney Harris...........
Hascaline Hamlin........
Jacob Hemlick...........
George S. Husted........
Charles Kinyon..........
Cassmer Komber..........
Henry Kirk..............
Jeremiah Kelley.........
Andrew Kennedy..........
James Kaagan............
Samuel Little...........
Edward H. Millington....
Charles Murrell.........
Luther Morgan...........
Richard Maitland........

Jonathan Macomber.......
Joseph McPherson........
Thos. I. McDonald.......
Lucius H. Mead..........
George Matterer.........
Bishop Marshall.........
Harvey Merrell..........
Bartholomew O'Sullivan
Peter Post..............
Henry Post..............
Author Page.............
Michael Ruf.............
Thomas Shiertcliff......
Leander Streeter........
Stephen Streeter........
Peter Sorbergg..........
Samuel V. Squares.......
John Souter.............
Jacob Souter............
Leonard B. Shears.......
Wm. H. Soper............
Earl W. Soper...........
Joseph E. Soule.........
David Steward...........
James Traynor...........
Charles Vhne............
John VanWormer..........
George Wheeler..........
Franklin Wilson.........
Wm. Wait................
Blise Wiser.............
Wm. Young...............
Lewis York..............

RECRUITS, NOVEMBER, 1861.

Geo. W. Atwell..........
Horace G. Bessey........
Alex Bennett............
Jasper Cheney...........

Wm. Conol...............
Alfred Dunster..........
Joseph Edmonds..........
George Ellis............

Square M. Gates.........
Peter Harland...........
John C. Hawley..........
M. D. Lyman.............

Ferdinand Livenson....
Chauncey McIntyre.....
Chauncey Minor..........
John F. Norton..........
Wm. H. Phipps..........
Luke Phipps.............
John Perrin.............

Charles Robinson........
Wm. Rawlinson..........
John Robertson..........
Geo. W. Rider...........
Leonard Sage............
George Strange..........
James Smart.............

Jacob Schenek...........
Abraham Wix.............
Jacob Webber............
Curtis Woodhall.........
George D. Wilson........
James Van Cise..........

RECRUITS, 1862.

David Arnold............
George Andrews..........
Robert Arnold...........
Henry Abbott............
Robert Bowers...........
Benj. W. Brabazon.......
Wm. H. Berritt..........
George Bouck............
Fred. K. Bewsher........
Lawrence L. Brown.......
Levi P. Blaker..........
Merrit L. Blasier.......
Maximillain Bellart.....
C. D. Campbell..........
Carlos F. Chadwick......
Albert Clark............
Frederick Clark.........
Hiram J. Cain...........
Chauncey H. Chapin......
Thomas Dean.............
John J. Davis...........
Edwin J. Dudley.........
Wm. Dale................
Seth D. Dunbar..........
James Donahue...........
Wm. Ford ....
C. M. Ford..............

Rileigh Gray............
Wm. M. Greenhill........
Oscar J. Gridley........
Cornelius Galvin........
Wm. H. Griffin..........
Luke E. Hitchcock.......
E. A. Gardiner..........
Eli Hicks...............
Julius Hazzard..........
James Hilton............
John Hall...............
John O. Follett.........
Daniel C. Follett.......
Robert Harrington.......
Hugh Hughes.............
George Jones............
Francis M. Lapham.......
John P. Little..........
A. M. Mills.............
Henry E. Morris.........
Thomas McGorden.........
Henry C. Minter.........
G. T. Murphy............
Ed. T. Montgomery.......
Frank V. Morey..........
Patrick Monnahan........
Chas. L. Mattison.......

Melvin E. Nichols.......
J. N. Newth.............
F. M. Parker............
John Peck...............
Lewis Robinson..........
Wm. Patterson...........
Thomas Robotham.........
Cornelius Ryan..........
Austin Randall..........
John W. Redner..........
Wm. Reilly..............
Michael Sullivan........
Edwin Segar.............
George H. Stewart.......
John S. Smith...........
Leroy Stebbins..........
John Stern..............
Truman Smith............
Dennis Sheean...........
Horace W. Sweet.........
Robert J. Tanner........
Chas. O. Townsend.......
G. W. Townsend..........
John Whipple............
Albert F. Wilcox........
Simeon H. Williams......

PROMOTIONS.

NAME.	Date of Commission	Date of rank	Remarks.
Colonels:			
Samuel J. Crooks........	Dec. 11, 1861	Nov. 28, 1861	Resigned Feb. 21, 1862.
Alfred Gibbs.............	Mar. 4, 1862	Mar. 4, 1862	Not mustered; declined.
Benjamin F. Davis......	June 7, 1862	June 6, 1862	Killed in action at Beverly Ford, Va., June 9, 1863.
William L. Markell......	Aug. 21, 1863	June 9, 1863	Not mustered; see Lieutenant Colonel.
William H. Benjamin, (*Bvt. Brig. Gen. U. S. V.*)	April 14, 1864	Feb. 27, 1864	Not mustered; declined; see Lieutenant Colonel.
Edmund M. Pope...... (*Bvt. Brig. Gen. U. S. V.*)	Feb. 25, 1865	Feb. 14, 1865	Mustered out with regiment June 27, 1865.
Lieut. Colonels:			
Charles R. Babbit........	Dec. 11, 1861	Nov. 28, 1861	Resigned March 23, 1863.
William L. Markell......	April 3, 1863	Mar. 23, 1863	Resigned Feb. 27, 1864,
William H. Benjamin...	Oct. —, 1863	June 9, 1863	Resigned Feb. 14, 1865.
Edmund M. Pope........	April 14, 1864	Feb. 27, 1864	Promoted to Colonel Feb. 25, 1865.
James Bliss............. (*Brevet Col. U. S. V.*)	April 13, 1864	April 13, 1865	Mustered out with regiment June 27, 1865.
Majors:			
Edmund M. Pope.....	Dec. 17, 1862	Dec. 1, 1862	Promoted to Lieut.-Colonel April 14, 1864.
William L. Markell......	Dec. 11, 1861	Nov. 28, 1861	Promoted to Lieut.-Colonel April 3, 1863.
Caleb Moore.............	June 23, 1863	Mar. 23, 1863	Mustered out, on expiration of term of service, Dec. 8, 1864.
William Downey........	April 13, 1865	April 13, 1865	Mustered out with regiment June 27, 1865.
William H. Benjamin....	Dec. 11, 1861	Nov. 28, 1861	Promoted to Lieut.-Colonel Oct. 1863.
James McNair...........	May 25, 1864	Mar. 1, 1864	Not mustered; see Captain.
James Bliss.............	Nov. 18, 1864	Oct. 31, 1864	Promoted to Lieut.-Colonel April 13. 1865.
Harmon P. Burroughs..	May 16, 1865	April 13, 1865	Mustered out with regiment June 27, 1865.
Albert L. Ford......... (*Bvt. Lt. Col. N. Y. V.*)	Apr. 14, 1864	Feb. 27, 1864	Not mustered; see Captain.
Hartwell B Compson.. (*Bvt. Lt. Col. N. Y. V.*)	Dec. 7, 1864	Nov. 20, 1864	Mustered out with regiment June 27, 1865.
Surgeons:			
James Chapman.........	Dec. 11, 1861	Oct. 9, 1861	Resigned Feb. 21, 1862.
Nelson D. Ferguson.....	Mar. 18, 1862	Mar. 7, 1862	Mustered out on expiration of term of service Dec. 8, 1864.
Peter E. Sickler..........	Dec. 9, 1864	Dec. 5, 1864	Mustered out with regiment June 27, 1865.

EIGHTH NEW YORK CAVALRY.

NAME.	Date of Commission	Date of rank	Remarks.
Assistant Surgeons:			
Winfield S. Fuller	Dec. 11, 1861	Nov. 28, 1861	Resigned Nov. 29, 1862.
Hiram D. Vosburg	Jan. 21, 1863	Jan. 16, 1863	Discharged Jan. 11, 1864.
Oscar H. Adams	May 12, 1864	May 7, 1864	Resigned Feb. 17, 1865.
Ebenezer H. Thurston	April 8, 1865	April 8, 1864	Mustered out with regiment June 27, 1865.
Eli K. Cole	April 17, 1863	April 17, 1863	Discharged Dec. 19, 1863.
George B. F. Simpson	Feb. 17, 1864	Feb. 10, 1864	Not mustered.
Charles G. Polk	May 13, 1865	May 12, 1865	Not mustered.
Regimental Adjt's:			
Albert L. Ford	Nov. 24, 1862	Sept. 30, 1862	Promoted to Captain Jan. 28, 1863.
E. B. Parsons	Aug. 14, 1863	Oct. 5, 1862	Promoted to Captain Oct. 7, 1863.
Charles T. Van Dusen	Feb. 13, 1864	Sept. 1, 1862	Promoted to Captain Feb. 17, 1865.
Henry C. Munn	Feb. 17, 1864	Feb. 6, 1865	Mustered out with regiment June 27, 1865.
Reg'tal Quar'masters:			
Frederick H. Barry			Discharged Jan. 22, 1862.
H. Orson Pope	Nov. 24, 1862	Sept. 30, 1862	Promoted to Captain April 18, 1864.
Albert S. Ford	Nov. 18, 1864	Nov. 14, 1864	Not mustered; declined.
Edward A. Bardwell	Feb. 17, 1865	Feb. 6, 1865	Mustered out with regiment June 27, 1865.
Battalion Adjutants:			
Frederick W. Clemens			See Second Lieutenant.
Edward H. Hunt	Mar. 26, 1862	Dec. 21, 1861	Discharged Sept. 22, 1862.
Frederick Scoville	Feb. 19, 1862	Nov. 27, 1861	Discharged Oct. 16, 1862.
Battalion Qm's:			
Theodore B. Hamilton			See Second Lieutenant.
William H. Webster			Promoted to First Lieutenant February 19, 1862.
Chaplains:			
John H. Van Ingen	Dec. 19, 1861	Nov. 18, 1861	Discharged Jan. 22, 1864; recommissioned.
John H. Van Ingen	Apr. 14, 1864	Jan. 22, 1864	Not mustered; declined.
Bethuel H. Braisted	Apr. 13, 1865	April 13, 1865	Mustered out with regiment June 27, 1865.
Reg'tal Commissaries:			
Edward H. Hunt	Nov. 24, 1862	Sept. 30, 1862	Not mustered; declined.
Rensselaer Gardner	June 23, 1862	Sept. 30, 1862	Mustered out with regiment June 27, 1865.
Captains:			
Edmund M. Pope	Dec. 11, 1861	Oct. 5, 1861	Promoted to Major Dec. 17, 1862.
Henry C. Cutler	June 23, 1863	Dec. 1, 1862	Not mustered; see First Lieutenant.
James Bliss	Aug. 14, 1863	June 25, 1863	Promoted to Major Nov. 18, 1864.
Charles T. Van Dusen	Feb. 17, 1865	Oct. 31, 1864	Mustered out with regiment June 27, 1865.

EIGHTH NEW YORK CAVALRY.

NAME.	Date of Commission	Date of rank	Remarks.
Caleb Moore............	Dec. 11, 1861	Oct. 5, 1861	Promoted to Major June 23, 1863.
Jacob Von Cedesston....	Aug. 21, 1863	Aug. 21, 1863	Not mustered; declined.
John J. McVean.........	April 14, 1864	Mar. 9, 1864	Promoted to Captain and A. A. G. August 20, 1864.
Harmon P. Burroughs..	Sept. 30, 1864	July 20, 1864	Promoted to Major May 16, 1865.
Andrew Kuder...........	May 31, 1865	April 13, 1865	Mustered out with regiment June 27, 1865.
John W. Dickenson......	Dec. 11, 1861	Oct. 5, 1861	Discharged Nov. 25, 1862.
Charles D. Follet........	Dec. 31, 1862	Dec. 29, 1862	Died July 4, 1863, of wounds received in action.
Enos B. Parsons.........	Oct. 7, 1863	July 1, 1863	Discharged April 20, 1864.
Richard S. Taylor.......	May 25, 1864	April 20, 1864	Not mustered; see First Lieutenant.
Elias VonRuger..........	July 27, 1864	July 15, 1864	Mustered out on expiration of term of service Dec. 8, 1864.
William Frisbie..........	Dec. 11, 1863	Oct. 5, 1861	Resigned Oct. 4, 1862.
Albert L. Ford...........	Jan. 23, 1861	Oct. 5, 1862	Mustered out on expiration of term of service Dec. 8, 1864.
Lewis V. Griffin.........	April 13, 1865	April 13, 1865	Not mustered; declined.
Benjamin F. Sisson......	Dec. 11, 1861	Oct. 16, 1861	Died of disease Feb. 11, 1863.
Benjamin C. Efner......	June 23, 1863	Feb. 11, 1863	Not mustered; see Second Lieutenant.
Murganzey Hopkins....	Aug. 14, 1863	June 25, 1863	Mustered out on expiration of term of service, Dec 8, 1864.
Robert E. Brewster......	Mar. 21, 1865	Mar. 24, 1865	Mustered out with regiment June 27, 1865.
Fennimar T. Gallett.....	Dec. 11, 1861	Oct. 12, 1861	Dismissed July 23, 1862.
Thomas Bell............. } (Brevet Maj. N. Y. V.) }	Aug. 1, 1862	July 5, 1862	Resigned April 28, 1863.
William H. Webster.....	Aug. 14, 1863	June 25, 1863	Not mustered; see First Lieutenant
Henry O. Pope..........	April 18, 1864	April 1, 1864	Discharged June 21, 1864.
Thomas S. Farr..........	Aug. 22, 1864	July 16, 1864	Died Oct., 1864.
Willard H. Healey.......	Feb. 19, 1862	Nov. 27, 1861	Resigned March 20, 1863.
Frederick Scoville.......	Aug. 14, 1863	June 25, 1863	Mustered out on expiration of term of service, Dec. 8, 1864.
John W. Davock........	Mar. 31, 1865	Mar. 31, 1865	Mustered out with regiment June 27, 1865.
John Wieland...........		Nov. 27, 1861	Discharged Oct. 27, 1862.
Hobert D. Mann.........		Sept. 1, 1862	Discharged March 26, 1863.
James A. Sayles.........	April 19, 1864	April 5, 1864	Killed in action at Nottoway, C. H., Va., June 23, 1864.
Asa L. Goodrich.........	June 1, 1864	April 23, 1864	Killed in action April 3, 1865.
Robert Nivin.............	May 31, 1865	April 13, 1865	Mustered out with regiment June 27, 1865.
Benjamin F. Foote.......	Dec. 11, 1861	Oct. 9, 1861	Killed in action at Beverly Ford, Va., June 9, 1863.
Charles McVean.........	Aug. 14, 1863	June 25, 1863	Died Oct. 26, 1864, at Macon, Ga., while a prisoner of war.
Dwight Hamilton......} (Brevet Maj. N. Y. V.) }	Nov. 18, 1864	Oct. 31, 1864	Mustered out with regiment June 27, 1865.

NAME.	Date of Commission	Date of rank	Remarks.
George H. Barry.........	Dec. 11, 1861	Oct. 23, 1861	Discharged Feb. 9, 1864.
Hartwell B. Compson...	Mar. 25, 1864	Feb. 9, 1864	Promoted to Major Dec. 7, 1864.
Jacob Chamberlain......	April 13, 1865	April 13, 1865	Not mustered; see First Lieutenant.
James McNair............	Nov. 1, 1862	Nov. 1, 1862	Killed in action June 23, 1864.
Reusselær Gardner......	June 30, 1865	April 13, 1865	Not mustered; see Regimental Commissary.
Vincent M. Smith........	Dec. 17, 1862	Oct. 6, 1862	Discharged Dec. 16, 1863.
Henry C. Frost..........	Jan. 20, 1864	Dec. 15, 1863	Mustered out on expiration of term of service Dec. 8, 1864.
George Matthews........	May 17, 1865	May 1, 1865	Mustered out with regiment June 27, 1865.
Selden E. Graves........	April 13, 1865	April 13, 1865	Mustered out with regiment June 27, 1865.
John N. Reeves..........	Feb. 18, 1865	Feb. 11, 1865	Mustered out with regiment June 27, 1865.
James W. Hooker........			Discharged Oct. 29, 1863.
First Lieutenants:			
Jasper B. Cheney........	April 14, 1864	Sep. 1, 1863	Discharged Dec. 5, 1864.
Ezra J. Peck.............	Dec. 11, 1861	Oct. 5, 1861	Resigned August 19, 1862.
Frederick Scoville.......	Oct. 23, 1862	Sep. 26, 1862	Promoted to Captain August 14, 1863.
Richard S. Taylor.......	Aug. 14, 1863	June 25, 1863	Killed in action May 14, 1864.
Andrew Kuder,..........	April 13, 1865	April 13, 1865	Promoted to Captain May 31, 1865.
George R. Achilles......	May 31, 1865	April 13, 1865	Mustered out with regiment June 27, 1865.
Frank O. Chamberlain..	Dec. 11, 1861	Oct. 16, 1861	Resigned August 13, 1862.
Samuel E. Sturtevant...	Nov. 24, 1862	July 22, 1862	Not mustered as First Lieutenant.
William C. Crafts........	Dec. 23, 1862	Nov. 26, 1862	Died August 29, 1863.
John W. Brown..........	Dec. 11, 1861	Dec. 5, 1861	Discharged Dec. 4, 1862.
John J. Brown...........	Oct. 7, 1863	Aug. 29, 1863	Mustered out on expiration of term of service Dec. 8, 1864.
Alfred Legett............	Mar. 30, 1865	Feb. 8, 1865	Mustered out with regiment June 27, 1865.
Thomas Bell.............	Dec. 11, 1861	Oct. 12, 1861	Promoted to Captain August 1, 1862.
Frederick W. Clemens..	Nov. 24, 1862	July 5, 1862	Not mustered; see Second Lieutenant.
James Bliss..............	June 23, 1863	Nov. 29, 1862	Promoted to Captain August 14, 1863.
Jervis W. Newton........	Aug. 14, 1863	June 25, 1863	Mustered out on expiration of term of service, Dec. 8, 1864.
Jacob Chamberlain......	Feb. 17, 1865	Feb. 6, 1865	Discharged May 30, 1865.
William H. Webster.....	Feb. 19, 1862	Nov. 27, 1861	Discharged Aug. 24, 1863.
Frederick Lansing, Jr..	Aug. 14, 1863	July 1, 1863	Discharged May 17, 1864.
Robert Niven............	April 8, 1865	Mar. 1, 1865	Promoted to Captain May 31, 1865.
C. Howard Beach........	May 31, 1865	April 13, 1865	Mustered out with regiment June 27, 1865.
John Schoen.............		Nov. 27, 1861	Resigned March 25, 1862.
Charles McVean.........		Sept. 1, 1862	Promoted to Captain August 14, 1863.

EIGHTH NEW YORK CAVALRY.

NAME.	Date of Commission	Date of rank	Remarks.
Harmon P. Burroughs..	Aug. 14, 1863	June 25, 1863	Promoted to Captain September 30, 1864.
Edgar C. Post............	Nov. 19. 1864	July 20, 1864	Mustered out with regiment June 27, 1865.
Alpha Whiton............	Dec. 11, 1861	Oct. 9, 1861	Resigned May 21, 1863.
George Matthews........	June 23, 1863	May 20, 1863	Mustered out on expiration of term of service Dec. 8, 1864, recommissioned.
Charles A. Goheen.......	April 13, 1865	April 13, 1865	Mustered out with regiment June 27, 1865.
Alfred S. Kinney........	Dec. 11, 1861	Oct. 23, 1861	Resigned August 21, 1862.
Adam C. Hogoboom.....	Nov. 24, 1862	Aug. 19, 1862	Resigned May 19, 1863.
Murganzey Hopkins....	June 23, 1863	May 20, 1863	Promoted to Captain August 14, 1863.
Carl Ludwig Berlin... (*Brevet Capt. U. S. V.*)	Nov. —, 1863	Oct. 6, 1863	Mustered out on expiration of term of service, Dec. 8, 1864.
Elias V. Ruger...........	April 7, 1864	April 7, 1864	Promoted to Captain July 27, 1864.
Horace B. Hooker.......	....	....	Resigned Oct. 25, 1862.
James McNair............	Oct. 27, 1862	Oct. 25, 1862	Promoted to Captain November 1, 1862.
John J. McVean.........	Nov. 1, 1862	Nov. 1, 1862	Promoted to Captain April 14, 1864.
Edward A. Bardwell.....	April 18, 1864	Mar. 24, 1864	Appointed Quartermaster.
Eugene A. Joslyn........	April 7, 1864	Mar. 20, 1864	Mustered out on expiration of term of service Dec. 8, 1864.
Hartwell B. Compson...	Aug. 14, 1863	June 25, 1863	Promoted to Captain March 25, 1864.
Morton A. Reed..........	Feb. 17, 1865	Feb. 6, 1865	Mustered out with regiment June 27, 1865.
Henry C. Frost..........	Dec. 17, 1864	Oct. 6, 1862	Promoted to Captain Jan. 20, 1864.
James P. Swain.........	April 14, 1864	Dec. 15, 1863	Died Dec. 20, 1864, in Hospital at Annapolis, Md.
George Matthews........	Feb. 17, 1865	Feb. 7, 1865	Promoted to Captain May 17, 1865.
Linsorff H. Carll........	May 31, 1865	May 1, 1865	Mustered out with regiment June 27, 1865.
William H. Osborn......	Feb. 17, 1865	Feb. 6, 1865	Mustered out with regiment June 27, 1865.
Samuel H. Bradley......	May 13, 1865	May 13, 1865	Not mustered.
John O. McCloskey......	Nov. 21, 1864	July 20, 1864	Discharged May 15, 1865.
James M. Seavers........	June 30, 1865	May 15, 1865	Not mustered; see Second Lieutenant.
George Skeels............	Dec. 28, 1864	Nov. 20, 1864	Mustered out with regiment June 27, 1865.
James B. Vanderholf	Dec. 18, 1862	Dec. 6, 1862	Resigned May 20, 1863.
Albert Huntington......	Aug. 14, 1863	June 25, 1863	Mustered out on expiration of term of service Dec. 8, 1864.
Alfred Leggett...........	Dec. 11, 1861	Oct. 5, 1861	Discharged August 13, 1863; recommissioned.
Henry C. Cutler.........	Dec. 11, 1861	Oct. 5, 1861	Killed in action at Beverly Ford, Va., June 9, 1863.
James E. Reeves.........	June 23, 1863	May 20, 1863	Not mustered as First Lieutenant.
John H. Osborn..........	Dec. 7, 1864	Dec. 7, 1864	Not mustered.

EIGHTH NEW YORK CAVALRY.

NAME.	Date of Commission	Date of rank	Remarks.
Second Lieutenants:			
Alfred E. Miller.........	Dec. 11, 1861	Oct. 9, 1861	Resigned May 17, 1862.
Henry Orson Pope......	July 18, 1862	May 14, 1862	Promoted to First Lieutenant and Quartermaster Nov. 24, 1862.
Alfred C. Worthley......	Dec. 10, 1862	Sept. 30, 1862	Discharged July 26, 1863.
Harvey A. Metcalf.......	Aug. 14, 1863	July 24, 1863	Mustered out on expiration of term of service Dec. 8, 1864.
Jacob Spoor..............	April 22, 1865	April 13, 1865	Mustered out with regiment June 27, 1865.
John A. Broadhead......	Dec. 11, 1861	Oct. 5, 1861	Resigned Dec. 26, 1862.
Murganzey Hopkins....	Jan. 28, 1863	Dec. 26, 1862	Promoted to First Lieutenant June 23, 1863.
Thomas S. Farr..........	Aug. 14, 1863	June 25, 1863	Promoted to Captain August 22, 1864.
Almon B. Strowger......	Aug. 22, 1864	July 16, 1865	Not mustered; declined.
John H. Reeves..........	Nov. 18, 1863	July 16, 1864	Promoted to Captain.
Frederick W. Clemons..	Dec. 11, 1861	Oct. 30, 1861	Resigned Nov. 26, 1862.
George Mathews.........	Dec. 10, 1862	Sept. 27, 1862	Promoted to First Lieutenant June 23, 1863.
Jasper B. Cheney........	Aug. 14, 1863	June 25, 1863	Promoted to First Lieutenant April 14, 1864.
George R. Achilles......	April 19, 1864	Mar. 25, 1864	Promoted to First Lieutenant May 31, 1865.
Albert L. Ford...........	Dec. 11, 1861	Oct. 14, 1861	Promoted to Regimental Adjutant Nov. 24, 1862.
R. James Colburn.......	Dec. 10, 1862	Sept. 27, 1862	Resigned June 5, 1863.
Dwight Hamilton.......	Aug. 14, 1863	June 25, 1863	Promoted to Captain, Nov. 18, 1864.
Charles H. Moody.......	Feb. 17, 1865	Oct. 31, 1864	Mustered out with regiment June 27, 1865.
Samuel E. Sturdevant...	Dec. 11, 1861	Oct. 16, 1861	Discharged Nov. 28, 1862.
James Bliss..............	April 3, 1863	July 22, 1862	Promoted to First Lieutenant June 23, 1863.
Carlos S. Smith..........	Aug. 14, 1863	June 25, 1863	Killed before muster.
George Skeels...........	Mar. 24, 1864	Mar. 23, 1864	Promoted to First Lieutenant Dec. 28, 1864.
Frank M. Parker........	Dec. 23, 1864	Dec. 1, 1864	Mustered out with regiment, June 27, 1865.
William M. Bristol......	Dec. 11, 1861	Oct. 17, 1861	Dismissed June 25, 1862.
James P. Swain..........	July 18, 1862	June 25, 1862	Promoted to First Lieutenant April 14, 1864.
Joseph Atwood..........	April 14, 1864	April 1, 1864	Not mustered; killed in action.
James M. Seavers.......	April 13, 1865	April 13, 1865	Mustered out with regiment June 27, 1865.
Frederick Scoville.......	Feb. 19, 1862	Nov. 27, 1861	See Battalion Adjutant.
Adam C. Hogoboom.....	Jan. 22, 1862	Nov. 28, 1861	Promoted to First Lieutenant, Nov. 24, 1862.
Rensselær Gardner......	Dec. 10, 1862	Sept. 27, 1862	Promoted to Regimental Commissary June 23, 1863.
Asa L. Goodrich.........	Aug. 14, 1863	June 25, 1863	Promoted to Captain, June 1, 1864.
Charles H. White........	Mar. 31, 1865	Mar. 31, 1865	Mustered out with regiment, June 27, 1865.
George Jachner.........		Nov. 27, 1861	Resigned March 25, 1862
E. Blossom Parsons.....		Sept. 1, 1862	Promoted to Regimental Adjutant Aug. 14, 1863.
C. Howard Beach........	April 13, 1865	April 13, 1865	Promoted to First Lieutenant May 31, 1865.

EIGHTH NEW YORK CAVALRY. 165

NAME.	Date of Commission	Date of rank	Remarks.
A. M. Mills...............	May 31, 1865	April 13, 1865	Mustered out with regiment June 27, 1865.
Theodore B. Hamilton...	Jan. 30, 1862	Nov. 19, 1861	Resigned June 11, 1862.
William C. Crafts.........	June 20, 1862	June 11, 1862	Promoted to First Lieutenant Dec. 23, 1862.
James E. Reeves..........	Jan. 28, 1863	Nov. 26, 1862	Died June 11, 1863, of wounds received in action.
Frederick Lansing......	June 29, 1863	June 23, 1863	Promoted to First Lieutenant Aug. 14, 1863.
Daniel E. Sackett........	Dec. 11, 1861	Oct. 23, 1861	Resigned Feb. 6, 1862.
Charles D. Follett.......	Feb. 24, 1862	Feb. 6, 1862	Promoted to Captain December 31, 1862.
Hartwell B. Compson...	April —, 1863	Dec. 29, 1862	Promoted to First Lieutenant March 25, 1864.
Samuel C. Fulton........	Feb. 10, 1864	Feb. 10, 1864	Mustered out with regiment June 27, 1865.
J. McNair...................			Promoted to First Lieutenant October 27, 1862.
Albert Huntington......	Oct. 27, 1862	Oct. 25, 1862	Promoted to First Lieutenant August 14, 1863.
Carl Ludwig Bertin.....	Oct. 7, 1863	Oct. 6, 1863	Promoted to First Lieutenant November, 1863.
Elias V. Ruger............	Mar. 15, 1864	Feb. 2, 1864	Promoted to First Lieutenant April 7, 1864.
Andrew Kuder............	July 27, 1864	July 15, 1864	Promoted to First Lieutenant April 13, 1865.
Benjamin C. Efner......	Dec. 17, 1862	Oct. 6, 1862	Died June 11, 1863, of wounds received in action at Beverly Ford, Va.
Lewis V. Griffin..........	Aug. —, 1863	April 17, 1863	Discharged July 22, 1864.
Lindorf H. Carll..........	Nov. 21, 1864	July 20, 1864	Promoted to First Lieut.
C. V. Beecher.............	May 31, 1865	May 1, 1865	Mustered out with regiment June 27, 1865.
Chester A. King..........	June 13, 1865	June 13, 1865	Not mustered.
B. F. Chappell.............	Feb. 18, 1865	Feb. 11, 1865	Not mustered; killed in action.
Jeremiah Hickman......	May 17, 1865	May 1, 1865	Mustered out with regiment June 27, 1865.
Milton Reynolds.........	May 31, 1865	April 13, 1865	Mustered out with regiment June 27, 1865.
A. M. Bristol..............	May 31, 1865	May 15, 1865	Mustered out with regiment June 27, 1865.
George V. Rider..........	Dec. 4, 1863	July 1, 1863	Discharged Feb. 1, 1864.
Eugene A. Joslyn........	Feb. 10, 1864	Feb. 1, 1864	Promoted to First Lieutenant April 7, 1864.
H. C. Bridges..............	July 27, 1864	July 15, 1864	Not mustered; declined.
Robert Niven.............	Nov. 18, 1864	July 15, 1864	Promoted to First Lieutenant April 8, 1865.
Charles A. Goheen......	April 8, 1865	Mar. 1, 1865	Promoted to First Lieutenant April 13, 1865.
Charles Cozean...........	April 13, 1865	April 13, 1865	Missing since April 20,1865.
E. P. Follett...............	April 13, 1865	April 13, 1865	Mustered out with regiment June 27, 1865.

BREVET COMMISSIONS ISSUED BY THE GOVERNOR TO ENLISTED MEN OF THIS REGIMENT.

RANK.	Name.	Brevet rank.
Corporal......................	Henry C. Carr...............	Second Lieutenant.

SURVIVORS.

FIELD OFFICERS.

William H. Benjamin, Colonel............................Rochester, N. Y.
William L. Markell, Colonel...................................Albany N. Y.
James Bliss, Colonel...Chicago, Ill.
H. B. Compson, Major...Chicago, Ill.
E. B. Parsons, Colonel.....................................Sodus Point, N. Y.
N. D. Ferguson, Surgeon.......................................Carthage, N. Y.

COMPANY A.

D. Hamilton, Capt....Louisville, Ky.
W. Webster, Capt..Central City, Neb.
George H. Allen......Rochester, N. Y.
Samuel Burrett....E. Hamilton, N. Y.
George W. Clark......Rochester, N. Y.
James Campbell........Webster, N. Y.
B. Hallings............Brighton, N. Y.
Wm. Keith............Rochester, N. Y.
Gottleib Konath......Rochester, N. Y.

Andrew Kuder.......S. Livonia, N. Y.
Wm. Kline............Rochester, N. Y.
Thomas Kanous...Pleasant Lake, Ind.
Wm. C. Kewin.........Rochester N. Y.
John Kirby..............Albion, N. Y.
George Reeder..........Penfield, N. Y.
John O'Neil.......Mingo Junction, O.
August Wagner.......Brighton, N. Y.
A. J. Nandee.......Williamston, Mich

COMPANY B.

Benj. Malben, 1st Sergt..Helena, M. T.
Horatio W. Smith.....So. Butler N. Y.
J. J. Brown..............Albion, N. Y.
P. M. Burton.....Honeoye Falls, N. Y.
F. S. Baldwin.........Rochester, N. Y.
A. H. Gates...............Lyons, N. Y.

J. A. Hickman.........Mt. Reed, N. Y.
Erastus Hanchett......E. Avon, N. Y.
Frank Haber............Parma, N. Y.
S. A. Roberts.....Honeoye Falls, N. Y.
R. M. Jones...........Neodesha, Kan.
John O. Follett........Norwich, N. Y.

COMPANY C.

M. Hopkins, Capt......Palmyra, N. Y.
M. Reynolds, 2d Lieut...Arkona, Can.
George B. Davis...Seneca Falls, N. Y.
John C. Hawley....Washington, D. C.
Lyman H. Essex......Brooklyn, N. Y.
George W. Harris....Newburgh, N. Y.
George N. Reeves........Marion, N. Y.

M. D. Sisson........Seneca Falls, N. Y.
G. Warner.............Palmyra, N. Y.
E. E. Hasner........Independence, Ia.
Sidney Stickels..........Waterloo, Ia:
Sol. Roberts......Honeoye Falls, N. Y.
J. C. Reeves..............Tampico, Ill.

COMPANY D.

Wm. B. Allen.........Rochester, N. Y.
A. E. Brooks.............Cleveland, O.
Lewis Gallaman..........Albion, N. Y.

W. E. Goodman......Rochester, N. Y.
David Knight............Sodus, N. Y.
Wm. Kelley...........Scottsville, N. Y.

EIGHTH NEW YORK CAVALRY.

Andrew Leggett......Rochester, N. Y.
Alfred Leggett.......Rochester, N. Y.
Fred Lansing........Watertown, N. Y.
O. E. Loomis..........Fairport, N. Y.
Robert B. Siddey....Poplar Hill, Kan.
Wm. Lovejoy............Menden, Mich.
Geo. S. Redfield....Chapinsville, N. Y.
Wm. Scholes..............Phelps, N. Y.
Robert H. Tripp........Waterloo, N. Y.
A. S. Wetmore...........Cleveland, O.
Linus B. Spoor..........Phelps, N. Y.
W. H. Story............Auburn, Dak.
Wm. Ford..........Preston, England
Albert Balcom.........Sherburne, N. Y.
Edward Benson.........German, N. Y.

COMPANY E.

Thomas Bell, Capt.....New York City
H. Alexander..........Lockport, N. Y.
H. H. Bickford..Johnson Creek, N. Y.
D. S. Brown...........Rochester, N. Y.
W. H. Davis...........Ridgeway, N. Y.
August Hawes.........Sanburn, N. Y.
John Hendrick........Rochester, N. Y.
Otis Humphrey........Palmyra, N. Y.
Oscar Hale...............Albion, N. Y.
John Robertson.........Buffalo, N. Y.
John B. Robson..Johnson Creek, N. Y.
J. K. Robson.....Johnson Creek, N. Y.
Eli Rogers..............Clyde, N. Y.
C. W. Roberts.........Walworth, N. Y.
Frank Wright........Brockport, N. Y.
John E. Ayers......Washington, D. C.

COMPANY F.

A. M. Mills, Lieut...Little Falls, N. Y.
A. W. Davis.............Waltham, Ia.
W. H. Phipps..........Shelbyville, Mo.
Joseph Elson.........Northville, Dak.
Robert A. Safford......Kingston, Pa.
Philip Spencer........Rochester, N. Y.
Dennis Sullivan....Strikerville, N. Y.
Frank Willett.............Flint, Mich.
W. H. Patterson......Rochester, N. Y.

COMPANY G.

Samuel Englis......Seneca Falls, N. Y.
Eli Hicks.........Oriskany Falls, N. Y.
Isaac Mapes..........Rochester, N. Y.
E. P. Roberts.........Rochester, N. Y.
Charles Stearns......Rushville, N. Y.
N. E. Evans.........Eau Claire, Wis.
J. E. Leigh..........Skaneateles, N. Y.
Isaac Tewkesburg.Seneca Falls, N. Y.
Wm. Logan..........Rochester, N. Y.
Nelson E. Evans........Banks, Mich.
O. F. Chamberlin..Canandaigua, N. Y.
Thomas Powers.......Cheshire, N. Y.
Avery Ingraham....Allen's Hill, N. Y.
Samuel English....Seneca Falls, N. Y.

COMPANY H.

F. W. Clemens, Capt......Orange, Cal.
A. S. Kinney, 1st Lieut.............
         North Norwich, N. Y.
D.E.Sackett,2d Lieut..Rochester,N.Y.
C. G. Hampton.........Detroit, Mich.
Nicholas Weiler........Hamlin, N. Y.
John Kehoe........Adams Basin, N. Y.
Van B. Crain..........Norwich, N. Y.
A. M. Dickenson..North Pitcher, N. Y.
George W. Brooks.....Norwich, N. Y.
Enos Guile...........Norwich, N. Y.
Walter B. Norton.....Norwich, N. Y.
Legard Norton........Norwich, N. Y.
Henry Norton.........Norwich, N. Y.
Andrew J. Terwilliger..Norwich, N. Y.
Louis Zimmeht......Great Bend, Kan.
Daniel D. Main..........Norwich, N. Y.
Wm. R. Guile.....Minneapolis, Minn.
Charles Geer..........Cortland, N. Y.
Benjamin Curtis........Sidney, N. Y.
Charles H. Graves......Franklin, N. Y.
John L. Church.......Sherburne, N. Y.
W. L. Conklin........Brockport, N. Y.
Edwin Day.............Bergen, N. Y.
Chas. W. Rapp........Rochester, N. Y.
H. McKee............Walworth, N. Y.
Smith Pratt............Ontario, N. Y.
Henry Post.......North Parma, N. Y.
E. J. Peck..............Phelps, N. Y.
Jacob Perrin.........Rochester, N. Y.
J. C. Vanderhoof.....Brockport, N. Y.
Wm. Vanlone...Penfield Centre, N. Y.

COMPANY I.

W. H. Healy, Capt......Blairsville, Pa.
John Schleger.........Webster, N. Y.
Fayette Allen..........Augusta, N. Y.
W. P. Sergeant.....Albert Lee, Minn.

George Schleger......Fairport, N. Y.
G. W. Sribburs.West Walworth, N. Y.
A. Buckinghan...........Phelps, N. Y.

Albert Camp...........Kirkland, N. Y.
Chas. O. Clark....Sauk Centre, Minn.

COMPANY K.

E. P. Follett, Capt....Rochester, N. Y.
George Brown.............York, N. Y.
H. F. Brooks.....Honeoye Falls, N. Y.
Wm. T. Brown........Rochester, N. Y.
Wm. Ball..............Caledonia, N. Y.
W. Bailey.............Walworth, N. Y.
Chas. H. Moody......Rochester, N. Y.
Henry C. Munn......Rochester, N. Y.
George Mathews.....Rochester, N. Y.
Edward Marriott......Louisville, Ky.
Martin Maylor........Rochester, N. Y.
John Noyes.............Albion, N. Y.
James Newton,..........Elston, Ind.

C. D. Owens.....Johnson Creek, N. Y.
Wm. Osborn...........Penfield, N. Y.
John Osborn..........Penfield, N. Y.
O. C. Palmer........Union Hill. N. Y.
Luke Phipps........Manchester, N. Y.
Wm. H. Patterson....Rochester, N. Y.
Thomas Posse..........Palmyra, N. Y.
Harry Robinson....Fowlerville, N. Y.
John Rose............Brockport, N. Y.
Henry M. Webb......Rochester, N. Y.
J. C. Havens...........Rochester N. Y.
Patrick O'Brien.....Montezuma, N. Y.
Fred Sinamus.........Fairport, N. Y.

COMPANY L.

A. Kuder, Capt......So. Livonia, N. Y.
F. J. Brown............ Penfield, N. Y.
D. B. Davis......Honeoye Falls, N. Y.
John J. DeGraw.....Mt. Morris, N. Y.
Wm. Logan...........Rochester, N. Y.
Fred Mate..............Geneseo, N. Y.
H. C. Livingston...Irondequoit, N. Y.
Wm. McKee............Charlotte, N. Y.
J. C. Havens..........Rochester, N. Y.
Peter Boyle.......Canandaigua, N. Y.

Francis Daily.....Minneapolis, Minn.
James Kelly..........Sottsville, N. Y.
Wm. Kelly............Sottsville, N. Y.
Wm. O. Raymond....Rochester, N. Y.
George Wright.........Geneseo, N. Y.
Jacob Leigler.........Palmyra, N. Y.
Nicholas H. Hoy...Spencerport, N. Y.
Chas. A. Goheen.Honeoye Falls, N. Y.
J. Kingelpager...Honeoye Falls, N. Y.

COMPANY M.

H. C. Frost, Capt.....Rochester, N. Y.
Jacob C. Andrews...Coldwater, Mich.
David Bruce..........Rochester, N. Y.
W. V. Barring........Flushing, Mich.
Richard Clinton...Spencerport, N. Y.
Josiah P. Davis.......Rochester, N. Y.
W. H. Fillman......E. Walworth, N. Y.
Robert Haslip............Greece, N. Y.
Lewis Gray..............Roxbury, Vt.

Daniel Hull..........E. Hamlin, N. Y.
David Hinman............Jeddo, N. Y.
Robert McGargo.........Holley, N. Y.
George Niner........Rochester, N. Y.
George Matthews....Mt. Morris, N. Y.
A. J. Whiting............Arcade, N. Y.
Earl W. Soper............Balbec, Ind.
Thos. Sweeney...E. Bloomfield, N. Y.
C. J. Mills...........Mt. Morris, N. Y.

KILLED IN ACTION.

NAME.	Grade.	Co.	Date of Death.	Place of death.
Davis, Benjamin F......	Colonel	—	June 9, 1863	Beverly Ford, Va.
Cary, John S............	Private	A	Sept. 16, 1864	Snickers Gap, Va.
Cook, Andrew J........	Private	A	June 9, 1863	Beverly Ford, Va.
Duell, Samuel H........	Sergeant	A	May 24, 1862	Berryville, Va.
Dunk, Harvey..........	Private	A	Nov. 12, 1864	Black Road, Va.
Edson, Albert H........	Corporal	A	July 1, 1863	Gettysburg, Pa.
Falkner, Robert........	Private	A	June 9, 1863	Beverly Ford, Va.
Lasson, John..........	Private	A	June 9, 1863	Beverly Ford, Va.
Rollinson, William.....	Corporal	A	April 1, 1865	Dinwiddie Court House, Va.
Schillinger, Jacob......	Private	A	Oct. 12, 1863	Brandy Station, Va.
Slocum, Edwin A.......	1st Sergt	A	July 1, 1863	Gettysburgh, Pa.
Bloss, John J..........	Q. M. S.	B	Sept. 19, 1864	Winchester, Va.
Bradburn, Thomas.....	Private	B	Aug. 25, 1864	Kearneysville, Va.
Cutler, Henry C........	1st Lieut	B	June 9, 1863	Beverly Ford, Va.
Edward, Isaac H.......	Corporal	B	April 3, 1865	Memodine Church, Va.
Gatens, Hugh..........	Private	B	Sept. 19, 1864	Winchester, Va.
Gilbert, Granville M...	Private	B	June 23, 1864	Nottoway Station, Va.
Hoag, Walter..........	Private	B	April 1, 1865	Five Forks, Va.
Lund, John............	Private	C	June 9, 1863	Beverly Ford, Va.
Robinson, Jackson.....	Sergeant	C	Nov. 10, 1862	Amesville, Va.
Aichinger, Christain...	Private	D	Sept. 16, 1864	Snickers Gap, Va.
Bowen, Nathan........	Private	D	April 1, 1865	Near Five Forks, Va.
Carr, Henry C.........	Private	D	Mar. 2, 1865	Waynestown, Va.
Church, Charles H.....	Sergeant	D	June 29, 1864	Near Stone Creek, Va.
Combs, Samuel H.....	Com Sur.	D	June 3, 1864	Near Salem Church, Va.
Cunningham, Patrick..	Private	D	April 8, 1865	....
Ford, Charles M.......	Private	D	June 9, 1863	Beverly Ford, Va.
Parsons, Linus........	Q. M. S.	D	June 23, 1864	Near Notterly Court House Va.
Bacon, Lyman.........	Private	E	Oct. 7, 1864	Columbia Furnace, Va.
Foote, Benjamin F.....	Captain	E	June 9, 1863	Beverly Ford, Va.
Garrett, James M.....	Private	E	Sept. 17, 1864	Snickers Gap, Va.
Hinman, Willis S......	Private	E	April 1, 1865	Five Forks, Va.
Kelley, Peter..........	Private	E	Nov. 6, 1862	Barber's Cross Roads, Va.
Smith, Carlos S.......	1st Sergt	E	Oct. 15, 1863	Broad Run, Va.
Taylor, Richard I......	1st Lieut	E	May 14, 1864	Strawberry Hill, Va.
Ware, Charles	Private	F	June 15, 1864	St. Mary's Church.
Donovan, Daniel.......	Private	F	Oct. 11, 1863	Stephansburg, Va.
Greene, Alfred D.......	Private	F	Feb. 6, 1864	Barnett's Ford, Va.
Sayles, James A.......	Captain	F	June 23, 1864	Nottoway Court House, Va.
Slater, Joseph.........	Private	F	July 9, 1863	Boonboro, Md.
Warner, James........	Sergeant	F	June 23, 1864	Near Nottoway Court House, Va.
Goodrich, Asa L.......	Captain	F	April 3, 1865	Anozoine Church, Va.
Smith, John S.........	Private	G	June 9, 1863	Beverly Ford, Va.

NAME.	Grade.	Co.	Date of Death.	Place of death.
Adams, William D......	1st Sergt	H	June 9, 1863	Beverly Ford, Va.
Townsend, George W..	1st Lieut	I	July 8, 1863	Boonsboro, Md.
Daniels, Robert.........	Private	K	Mar. 4, 1863	On picket near Independence Hill, Va.
Foss, Jacob.............	Private	K	Feb. 7, 1864	Burnett's Ford, Va.
McKenzie, Andrew.....	Private	K	Mar. 4, 1863	Independence Hill, Va.
Stumpf, John...........	Captain	K	June 19, 1862	....
Baldwin, H. B..........	Private	L	May 12, 1864	Meadow Bridge.
Brewster, Charles H....	Private	L	June 10, 1863	Beverly Ford, Va.
McKeown, James E.....	Corporal	L	Aug. 1, 1863	Near Brandy Station, Va.
McNair, James..........	Captain	L	June 23, 1864	Nottoway Court House, Va.
White, Silas............	Private	L	July 10. 1863	Funkstown, Md.
Macomber, Jonathan..	Private	M	July 2, 1863	Gettysburg, Pa.
Traynor, James.........	Private	M	Feb. 6, 1864	Barnett's Ford, Va.

DEATHS FROM WOUNDS RECEIVED IN ACTION.

NAME.	Grade.	Co.	Date of Death.	Remarks.
Daggert, Horace W....	Sergeant	A	April 21, 1865	Alexandria, Va., gun shot wound.
Van Tama, John R.....	Sergeant	A	July 5, 1864	In hospital, Buffalo, N. Y.
Burgess, Edwin S......	Private	B	June 13, 1864	Of wounds received at White Oak Swamp, Va.
Canfield, John.........	Private	B	Mch. 15, 1865	Rebel prison, Andersonville, Va.
Hess, James............	Private	B	July 1, 1864	Prince George Court House hospital.
King, Marshall H......	Private	B	May 11, 1865	April 8, 1865, wounds received.
Ludding, John.........	Private	B	June 24, 1862	Of disease at Harper's Ferry.
McGrath, John.........	Private	B	Sept. 22, 1864	Of disease at Giesboro.
Pason, Albert..........	Private	B	Aug. 11, 1863	Of disease at Relay House Md.
Robb, Alonzo B........	Corporal	B	Dec. 25, 1864	Of disease at general hospital.
Rabotham, Thomas....	Private	B	Nov. 25, 1862	Of disease at Hagerstown.
Slade, William.........	Private	B	Dec. 30, 1861	Of disease at Washington, D. C.
Taft, Robert............	Corporal	B	Dec. 29, 1861	Of disease at Columbia hospital.
Taylor, Martin J.......	Corporal	B	Aug. 10, 1862	Of disease at Relay House, Md.
Treadwell, Orsin.......	Private	B	Jan. 21, 1862	Of disease at Meriden Hill, D. C.
Weaver, Chester........	Private	B	Oct. 17, 1864	Of disease at Camp Parol hospital, Annapolis, Md.
Welkley, Samuel.......	Private	B	July 30, 1864	Of disease at Andersonville, Ga.
Winnet, Joseph A......	Private	B	Mch. —, 1865	Rebel prison, Andersonville, Ga.
Witherill, John........	Private	B	Oct. 6, 1864	Rebel prison, Andersonville, Ga.
Woodman, Walter......	Sergeant	B	Aug. 25, 1864	Kearneysville, Va.
Ades, Edward..........	Private	C	June 7, 1864	Andersonville, Ga. prisoner.
Allen, Eli H............	Private	C	Sept. 23, 1862	Harpers Ferry, Md., of disease.
Barnes, Calder.........	Private	C	May 27, 1865	In hospital at Baltimore, Md.
Brown George.........	Private	C	Feb. 26, 1862	In hospital at Washington, D. C.

NAME.	Grade.	Co.	Date of Death.	Remarks.
Clark, George A........	Corporal	C	Jan. 10, 1863	In hospital at Bell Plain, Va.
Dumell, Elijah..........	Private	C	Jan. 20, 1862	In hospital of disease, Washington, D. C.
Failing, Milton M......	Private	C	May 7, 1865	At Macon, Ga., taken prisoner.
Goodrich, George......	Private	C	Feb. 20, 1863	Regimental Hospital, Bell Plain, Va.
Lennox, Samuel........	Private	C	May 29, 1864	Hospital, Craig's Church, Va.
Reeves, James E........	2d Lieut	C	June 10, 1863	Georgetown, D. C.
Follett, Henry D.......	Captain	D	July 4, 1863	Of wounds received at Gettysburg, Pa.
Marsh, Henry D........	Private	D	Sept. 27, 1863	Lincoln Hospital, Washington, D. C., of wounds.
Byers, John..............	Private	E	June 12, 1863	Washington, D. C.
Griffin, Henry..........	Private	E	Nov. 19, 1862	Fredericksburg, Md.
Doran, John.............	Private	F	May 19, 1864	Spot'sylvania Court House, Va.
McFarland, John.......	Private	H	May 25, 1862	Winchester, Va.
Bronson, William......	Private	I	July 23, 1863	G. H., Frederick City, Md.
Butler, Samuel.........	Sergeant	I	Oct. 12, 1863	Stevensburg, Va.
Efner, Benjamin C.....	2d Lieut	I	June 12, 1863	Georgetown, D. C., in hospital.
Shaffer, Sylvester......	Private	I	July 6, 1864	City Point Hospital, Va.
Wade, Mortimer E.....	Private	K	Oct. 11, 1863	Stevensburg, Va.
Culver, Milton..........	Corporal	M	June 21, 1863	Of wounds.
Kennedy, Andrew......	Private	M	June 15, 1864	White Oak Swamp.
McPherson, Joseph....	Corporal	M	Oct. 12, 1863	....

DEATHS FROM DISEASE AND OTHER CAUSES.

NAME.	Grade.	Co.	Date of Death.	Remarks.
Dodge, John S...........	Com.Ser.	—	July 6, 1862	Of typhoid fever, at Relay House.
Sickler, Peter E.........	Surgeon	—	April 14, 1865	Of chronic diarrhœa, in the field.
Arnst, Robert M.........	Private	A	Jan. 28, 1865	At Salisbury, N. C. while a prisoner.
Barber, Alfred W.......	....	A	....	Taken prisoner at Beverly Ford, Va., June 9, 1863.
Buck, Nathan............	Private	A	April 14, 1863	Of disease at Potomac Creek, Va.
Cane, Reuben............	Private	A	July 30, 1864	At Andersonville, Ga., prisoner of war.
Carnell, Charles.........	Private	A	April 5, 1863	At Hope Landing, Va., of disease.
Case, Abel F.............	Private	A	Sept. 11, 1864	At Andersonville, Ga., prisoner of war.
Daggett, John...........	....	A	Sept. 28, 1864	At Waynesboro, Va., probably as a prisoner.
Dailey, John J...........	Private	A	July 19, 1863	In hospital at Washington, D. C. of disease.
DeMaille, J. Peter.......	Private	A	April 27, 1862	At Edwards Ferry, Md. of disease.
Dibble, George O.......	Private	A	Sept. 16, 1863	In hospital at Washington, D. C., of disease.
Dikeman, Robert B.....	Private	A	Dec. 16, 1861	In hospital at Washington, D. C., of disease.
Doubleday, Jerome M..	Sergeant	A	May 17, 1862	At Harpers Ferry, Va., of disease.
Duty, Walter T..........	Private	A	....	At Andersonville Ga., prisoner of war.
Elson, Thomas...........	Private	A	April 11, 1865	At Carlton, N. Y., of disease.
Gardiner, Edwin E.....	Private	A	Mar. 8, 1865	At Annapolis, Md., a paroled prisoner.
Hill, William.............	Private	A	Jan. 2, 1865	At Salisbury, N. C., of diarrhœa.
Hubbard, John..........	Private	A	Jan. 5, 1865	At Salisbury, N. C., while a prisoner of war.
Knapp, Robert...........	Private	A	Oct. 11, 1864	At Salisbury, N. C., while a prisoner of war.
Lothrop, William C....	Sergeant	A	Sept. 7, 1862	At Marine Hospital, Baltimore, Md., of disease.
McCormac, John.......	Private	A	Mar. 25, 1862	In hospital at Washington, D. C., of disease.
McVean, Charles.......	Captain	A	Sept. 11, 1864	At Charlestown, S. C., while a prisoner of war.

NAME.	Grade.	Co.	Date of Death.	Remarks.
Manchester, Augustus.		A		Captured, not heard from since.
Miller, John A.	Private	A	Jan. 2, 1864	At Richmond, Va., a prisoner of war.
Northrup, Needham.	Private	A	1865	Date unknown.
O'Brian, William.	Private	A	June 2, 1864	At Andersonville, Ga., a prisoner of war.
Schulick, John.		—		Appointed Sergeant March 10, 1863, captured August 1, 1863, at Brandy Station, Va.
Scout, Isaac.	Private	A	Feb. 13, 1862	In hospital at Washington, D. C., of disease.
Segar, Edward E.	Private	A	Sept. 28, 1864	At Andersonville, Ga., of disease.
Smith, Nathan.	Private	A	April 13, 1864	At his home in Chenango Co., N. Y.
Voorhees, Edward M.	Corporal	A	Nov. 11, 1864	At Florence, S. C., while a prisoner of war.
Averel, Henry.	Private	B	Mch. 3, 1862	Of disease in hospital at Washington, D. C.
Baker, Horace A.	Private	B	Dec. 28, 1862	Of disease, Bedloe's Island, N. Y. Hospital.
Bell, Myron A.	Private	B	June 16, 1864	Of disease at Cavalry Corps Hospital.
Bell, Stewart H.	Corporal	B	July 16, 1863	At McVeigh House, branch hospital.
Clark, Frederick.	Private	B	July 6, 1864	Andersonville, Ga., in rebel prison.
Connors, Christopher.	Private	B	Nov. 23, 1863	Of disease at Washington, D. C.
Daniels, Celon A.	Private	B	Dec. 18, 1864	In hospital at Winchester, Va.
Daniels, Timothy H.	Private	B	Mch. 15, 1863	Of disease.
Darcey, Charles.	Private	B	June 25, 1862	Of disease in hospital.
Doxey, William.	Private	B	Oct. 12, 1864	At Andersonville, Ga.
Follett, Daniel.	Private	B	July 26, 1864	At Andersonville, Ga.
Ford, Whitcomb.	Private	B	Oct. 10, 1864	Of disease Camp Parol, Annapolis, Md.
Jump, Orrin.	Private	B	Sept. 17, 1864	At Andersonville, Ga.
Harrington, Dorian T.	Bl'ks'th	C	Feb. 2, 1863	Accidental poisoning, White Oak Church, Va.
Hurgate, George.	Private	C	Feb. 18, 1862	Of disease at Washington, D. C.
Knickerbocker, H. P.	Private	C	Mch. 16, 1865	At Annapolis, Md., prisoner of war.
McKinney, Robert.	Private	C	Mch. 20, 1863	Of disease near Stafford Court House, Va.
O'Niel, Edward.	Private	C	Feb. 14, 1864	At Camp Stone, D. C., gun shot wound.
Robinson, Edwin K.	Q. M. S.	C	June 30, 1862	Of disease at Harper's Ferry.
Stace, Charles.	Private	C	Aug. 18, 1862	Of disease at Regimental Hospital, Relay House, Va.
Stern, John.	Private	C	Oct. 18, 1864	Of accidental drowning at City Point, Va.
Swain, James P.	1st Lieut	C	Dec. 20, 1864	Of disease at general hospital, Annapolis, Md.
Sweet, Louis H.	Private	C	June 23, 1865	Of disease at Washington, D. C.

EIGHTH NEW YORK CAVALRY. 175

NAME.	Grade.	Co.	Date of Death.	Remarks.
Taylor, William H......	Private	C	Dec. 3, 1864	Of disease.
VanWormer, Edwin S..	Private	C	May 7, 1862	Of disease at Harpers Ferry, Va.
Anderson, Homer......	Private	D	Dec. 12, 1862	Of disease at Bell Plain, Va.
Bannister, Thaddeus...	Private	D	....	While prisoner of war.
Bedford, Francis.......	Private	D	April 22, 1862	Of disease at Elmira, N. Y.
Blackman, Wallace.....	Corporal	D	Feb. 16, 1862	Of disease at Columbian Hospital, D. C.
Brown, Gilbert..........	Private	D	Oct. 1, 1864	In prison at Andersonville, Ga.
Campbell, Daniel.......	Farrier	D	May 20, 1864	In prison at Andersonville, Ga.
Davis, John J...........	Private	D	Mar. 28, 1864	U. S. General Hospital, Annapolis, Md.
Dobson, Isaac J.........	Private	D	Oct. 29, 1862	At hospital, Hagerstown, Md.
Donnelly, Chas. A......	Private	D	Nov. 9, 1863	At N. Y. Soldiers' Home, of disease.
Edwards, Benjamin....	Private	D	Feb. 17, 1863	At Regimental Hospital near Stafford Court House, Va.
German, William.......	Private	D	Oct. 12, 1864	At Andersonville, Ga., of disease.
Gridley, Oscar J. Jr....	Private	D	Nov. 14, 1862	At Frederick, Md, of disease.
Hannahs, James........	Private	D	July 23, 1864	Taken prisoner at Amosville, Va.
Harvey, Barton J.......	Private	D	....	At Miller, Ga., while a prisoner of war.
Hicks, James D.........	Corporal	D	Feb. 23, 1862	At Columbian College Hospital, Washington, D. C.
Pettibone, Eli F........	Private	D	Feb. 15, 1865	At Florence, S. C., of starvation.
Pierce, Darwin H......	Private	D	Oct. 30, 1864	At Andersonville, Ga., of scorbutis.
Plaford, James W......	Private	D	....	In Georgia, while prisoner of war.
Pulis, Daniel W.........	Private	D	Mar. 27, 1865	At Clarendon, N. Y., of disease.
Rupert, Albert B........	Sergeant	D	Mar. 18, 1864	At Andersonville, Ga., of disease.
Scott, Stephen D........	Private	D	Oct. —, 1864	While prisoner of war.
Smith, Edson...........	Private	D	Dec. 1, 1861	At Washington, D. C., of disease.
Smith, Joseph D........	Private	D	Sept. 3, 1864	In insane asylum, Washington, D. C.
Spoor, Cornelius........	Private	D	Jan. 20, 1865	At Phelps, N. Y.
Wood, Daniel...........	Private	D	April 5, 1862	At Edwards' Ferry, Md., of disease.
Wood, John.............	Private	D	April 6, 1862	At Edwards' Ferry, Md., of disease.
Allen, Henry............	Private	E	....	Andersonville, Ga.
Atwood, Joseph........	Sergeant	E	....	Prisoner of war.
Barton, Alexander.....	Private	E	Sept. 10, 1862	At Baltimore, Md., of disease.
Beckwith, Adolphus A..	Private	E	Nov. 24, 1862	At Washington, D. C., of disease.
Clapp, Asa F............	Private	E	Nov. 16, 1862	Of disease at Rappahannock, Va.
Coates, William........	Private	E	Feb. 24, 1863	Of disease at Bell Plain, Va.
Crafts, William C......	1st Lieut	E	Aug. 29, 1863	....

EIGHTH NEW YORK CAVALRY.

NAME.	Grade.	Co.	Date of Death.	Remarks.
Fearby, F. William.....	Bugler	E	....	At Andersonville, Ga., of disease.
Fisk, Newton............	Private	E	June 29, 1862	Charleston, Va., of disease.
Hunter, Samuel........	Private	E	Aug. 10, 1864	At Richmond, Va., while prisoner of war.
Johnson, James........	Private	E	Aug. 15, 1862	Of disease at Relay House, Md.
Lathrop, Henry H......	Q. M. S.	E	Feb. 7, 1862	Of disease at Brockport, N. Y.
Marvin, James H.......	1st Sergt	E	Mch. 12, 1862	Of disease at Washington, D. C.
Morey, Frank H........	Private	E	Oct. 19, 1864	At Andersonville, Ga. while a prisoner of war.
Pierce, Otis W..........	Private	E	May 23, 1865	Of disease at Washington, D. C.
Purdy, Wm. F..........	Private	E	Mch. 12, 1862	Of disease near Stafford's Court House, Va.
Smith, Orrin............	Private	E	May 24, 1862	Of disease at Charleston, Va.
Van Orman, Isaac......	Private	E	Oct. 28, 1864	Of disease at Andersonville, Ga.
Wallace, Charles.......	Private	E	Sept. 20, 1862	Of disease at Baltimore, Md.
Watterson, James......	Private	E	Mch. 13, 1862	Of disease in hospital at Washington, D. C.
Watton, Elijah.........	Private	E	....	Of disease in hospital at Andersonville, Ga.
Woodhull, David K.....	Private	E	....	Of disease in hospital at Andersonville, Ga.
Beane, Geo. B..........	Private	F	Sept. 13, 1862	Of typhoid fever at Harpers Ferry, Va.
Bonnett, Wesley M.....	Private	F	Feb. 23, 1862	Of typhoid fever at Washington, D. C.
Campbell, C. D.........	Private	F	Dec. 25, 1862	Of pneumonia at Washington, D. C.
Kellogg, Lewis F.......	Private	F	Dec. 26, 1863	Of pneumonia at Richmond, Va.
Robbins, Lysander L..	Private	F	April 23, 1862	Of disease at Summit House, H. Philadelphia, Pa.
Rose, Abraham.........	Private	F	Aug. 11, 1863	Of typhoid pneumonia at Fort Wood.
Tower, John H.........	Private	F	May 1, 1862	Of fever at Harpers Ferry, Va.
Van Cise, James........	Bugler	F	Mch. 15, 1862	Of disease at Washington, D. C.
Vitty, George...........	Private	F	Mch. 1, 1863	Of dropsy at Bell Plain, Va.
Waters, Alanson L.....	Private	F	Oct. 4, 1864	Of dysentery at Andersonville, Ga.
Blair, James............	Corporal	F	Jan. 16, 1864	While a prisoner of war at Andersonville, Ga.
Casey, Jeremiah........	Corporal	F	Nov. 25, 1864	While a prisoner of war at Florence, S. C.
Cone, Lewis............	Private	F	Mch. 9, 1864	....
Donahue, Daniel.......	Sergeant	F	Oct. 29, 1864	....
Hall, William...........	Private	F	Sept. 23, 1864	At Andersonville, Ga., of starvation.
Lewis, Benjamin.......	Private	F	Jan. 5. 1865	At Rush. N. Y., on parol.
Raines, John S.........	Q. M. S.	F	....	At Annapolis, Md., of diarrhœa.
Rockfellow, C. C........	Private	F	Oct. 25, 1864	At Florence, S. C., while a prisoner of war.

NAME.	Grade.	Co.	Date of Death.	Remarks.
Vaughn, Wm. H.	Private	F	June 7, 1864	Andersonville, Ga., while prisoner of war.
Walker, James	Private	F	Oct. 8, 1864	At Charleston, S. C., while prisoner of war.
White, Clark	Corporal	F	Mch. 16, 1864	At sea.
Bassett, Oscar J.	Corporal	G	Aug. 16, 1862	Typhoid fever R. H. Relay House, Md.
Bockoren, Peter W.	Corporal	G	Aug. 26, 1863	Malarial fever, Washington, D. C.
Cooley, Ia. M.	Private	G	June 5, 1863	Of disease at Acquia Creek, Va.
Crafts. Wm. C.	1st Lieut	G	Aug. 29, 1863	Weaversville, Va.
Dweller, E. Delafied	Corporal	G	Dec. 20, 1861	Of consumption at Rushville.
Gustin, Aaron	Private	G	Mch. 18, 1864	Rubeola, Albany, N. Y.
Hazard, Julius	Private	G	Oct. 22, 1863	Typhoid pneumonia, at Hagerstown, Md.
Knickerbocker, Miles	Private	G	Nov. 12, 1862	Gunshot wound, R. Hospital.
King, Daniel	Private	G	Feb. 25, 1862	Typhoid fever, G. H. Washington, D. C.
Leigh, Joseph E.	Private	G		Wounded Oct. 11, 1863.
Notterville, Wm.	Blksmth	G	Oct. 1, 1864	While prisoner of war at Andersonville, Ga.
Page, Wm. H. H.	Sergeant	G	Nov. 1, 1862	Government Hospital No. 2, Frederick, Md.
Sisson, Benj. T.	Captain	G	Feb. 11, 1863	Congestion of lungs, Bell Plain, Va.
Smith, Levi R.	Private	G	Jan. 28, 1863	Congestive fever, Washington, D. C.
Travis, Horton	Private	G	Aug. 29, 1864	Andersonville, Ga.
Bailey, James	Private	G	Jan. 30. 1865	Baltimore, Md., of disease.
Boyle, Thomas	Private	G	Nov. 9, 1864	While prisoner of war at Andersonville, Ga.
Carraher, John	Private	G	Oct. —, 1864	Supposed while prisoner of war at Andersonville Ga.
Foger, Frederick W.	Private	G	May 20, 1865	Erysipelas, at Washington, D. C.
Hammond, D. C.	Private	G	Nov. 4, 1864	Of disease near Strasburgh Va.
Henry, William	Private	G	July 27, 1865	Of disease, Government Hospital, Alexandria, Va.
Selleck, Noah	Private	G		While prisoner of war.
Tefft, Moses	Private	G	April 17, 1865	Typhoid fever, Camp Parole, Md.
Atwell, Geo. W.	Private	H	July 31, 1862	Relay House, of disease.
Barnes, Stephen A.	Private	H	Feb. 27, 1863	Typhoid fever, Relay House Bell Plain, Va.
Beasley, Edmund	Private	H	Sept. 15, 1862	Typhoid fever at Harper's Ferry, Va.
Beckwith, Edward E.	Corporal	H	Jan. 21, 1863	Bell Plain, Va.
Chase, Howard L.	Private	H	Mch. 15, 1862	Of disease at Washington, D. C.
Church, Milo	Private	H	Jan. 6, 1862	Of disease at Washington, D. C.
Church, Samuel	Private	H	Feb. 16, 1862	Of disease at Washington, D. C.
Cook, Walter	Private	H	Feb. 22, 1862	
Copeland, John	Private	H	Aug. 23, 1862	Of disease at Relay House, Md.

EIGHTH NEW YORK CAVALRY.

NAME.	Grade.	Co.	Date of Death.	Remarks.
Cotton, Wm. H.........	Private	H	Mch. 25, 1863	Of disease at Hope Landing, Va.
Emmonds, Henry B....	Private	H	April 14, 1863	....
Foote, George..........	Private	H	Dec. 20, 1861	Of disease at Washington, D. C.
Harrington, Robert....	Private	H	July 26, 1864	Of disease at Camp Stoneman, Washinton, D. C.
Lovejoy, Henry........	Private	H	Nov. 25, 1861	At his home in Spencerport, N. Y., of disease.
McFarland, Charles....	Private	H	April 11, 1862	At Edwards Ferry, Va., of disease.
Paul, Edwin B..........	Private	H	Jan. 23, 1864	At Convalescent Camp, Va.
Rhodes, George.........	Private	H	Feb. 22, 1862	At Washington, D. C., of disease.
Scott, Albert............	Private	H	Feb. 23, 1862	At Washington, D. C., of disease.
Carruthers, Alexander	Corporal	H	Oct. 3, 1864	Charleston, S. C., while prisoner of war.
Case, Edward...........	Private	H	Sept. 10, 1864	At Andersonville, Ga., of disease.
Chappell, Benj. F.......	Sergeant	H	April 21, 1865	At Washington, D. C.
Gleisle, Julius..........	Private	H	April 17, 1865	At Washington, D. C., from gunshot wound.
Hanes, Volney S........	Private	H	July 27, 1864	Andersonville, Ga.
Hosmer, George........	Private	H	Sept. 10, 1864	Andersonville, Ga., while prisoner of war.
Hotchkiss, Albert G....	Private	H	Aug. 27, 1864	In hospital at Andersonville, Ga.
Reddy, Peter............	Private	H	Oct. 31, 1864	While prisoner of war at Andersonville, Ga.
Shipper, John..........	Private	H	Aug. 19, 1865	While prisoner of war at Andersonville, Ga.
Snyder, John...........	Private	H	June 6, 1865	Of disease at Baltimore, Md.
Zainper, Frank.........		H	....	Died in rebel prison, place and date of death not known.
Burliston, John A......	Private	I	Dec. 6, 1862	At Hagerstown, Md., of disease.
Heith, Henry...........	Private	I	Sept. 12, 1863	Of gunshot wounds.
Hoag, John W..........	Private	I	Sept. 19, 1863	Of disease at Harper's Ferry, Va.
Jeffery, Henry..........	Private	I	Feb. 1, 1862	Of disease at Washington, D. C.
Kirkwood, John........	Private	I	Feb. 8, 1862	Of disease at Washington, D. C.
Lawrence, David.......	Private	I	Mar. 9, 1863	Of disease at Dumfries, Va.
Livermore, Fernando..	Private	I	Oct. 11, 1863	Of disease at Washington, D. C.
Morey, Frank W........	Private	I	Oct. 19, 1864	While prisoner of war at Andersonville, Ga.
Peck, John..............	Private	I	Oct. 3, 1864	Of disease at Giesboro, D.C.
Scribner, Elam.........	Corporal	I	Jan. 10, 1863	Of disease at Adrian, Mich.
Strong, Myron..........	Private	I	May 13, 1864	At Richmond, Va., while prisoner of war.
Sykes, James...........	Private	I	July 6, 1862	At Relay House, Md., of disease.
Utley, Alpha............	Private	I	Dec. 24, 1861	Of smallpox at Washington, D. C.
Armstrong, Daniel.....	Private	K	April 6, 1868	Of wounds.
Blair, James............	Corporal	K	July 16, 1865	Of disease at Andersonville, Ga.

EIGHTH NEW YORK CAVALRY.

NAME.	Grade.	Co.	Date of Death.	Remarks.
Calder, Daniel............	Private	K	April 6, 1863	Of disease.
Gage, Daniel.............	Teamst'r	K	Nov. 2, 1862	Cause of death not given.
Giescan, Daniel..........	....	K	....	....
Hahn, Henry.............	Private	K	Oct. 5, 1863	Of disease.
Lewis, Benjamin F......	Private	K	Jan. 2, 1865	Annapolis, Md.
Lutes, Peter..............	Private	K	June 8, 1863	Of disease.
McNaughton, William..	Private	K	May 2. 1863	Of disease.
McNaughton, William..	Com.Ser.	K	Aug. 26, 1863	Of disease.
McVean, Daniel J......	Private	K	Oct. 25, 1863	Of disease.
Powell, Duane............	Corporal	K	April 23, 1863	Of disease.
Raines, John T..........	Q. M. S.	K	Dec. 18, 1864	Of disease.
Salmon, William........	Private	K	Mar. 4, 1863	Of disease.
Scott, Geo. B.............	Corporal	K	July 2, 1863	Of gunshot wound.
Vaughn, Wm. H.........	Private	K	June 17, 1864	Of disease at Andersonville hospital.
Cogswell, Watson........	Private	L	April 22, 1865	Of disease.
Bailey, James.............	Private	L	Jan. 30, 1865	Of disease.
Boyle, Thomas...........	Private	L	Nov. 9, 1864	No cause stated.
Canagher, John.........	Private	L	Oct. —, 1864	Supposed to have died about last of October.
Farr, Thos. L.............	Captain	L	....	While prisoner of war at Charlottsville, Va.
Hammond, D. C.........	Private	L	Nov. 4, 1864	Of disease.
Hunt, Wm................	Q. M. S.	L	Sept. 7, 1864	At Baltimore, Md., of disease.
McDowall, Enos.........	Corporal	L	Nov. 2, 1862	Of disease.
Buckley, Philip..........	Private	M	June 22, 1864	Of gunshot wound, Hampton, Va.
Case, Edward............	Private	M	Sept. 10, 1864	Of disease at Andersonville prison.
Gleason, William........	Private	M	Sept. 2, 1863	Of disease.
Gott, Edward.............	Private	M	Mar. 25, 1863	Of disease.
Hicks, Jno. H. M. N....	Private	M	Mar. 30, 1864	Of disease.
Michner, H. P............	....	M	Feb. 11, 1865	Salisbury, N. C.
Pike, Titus H............	Private	*	April 24, 1863	At Washington, D. C., of pneumonia.

*Unassigned.

NAMES AND DATES OF ENGAGEMENTS.

Winchester, Va., May 25th, 1862........
Harpers Ferry, September 14th, 1862..
Antietam, Md. September 17th, 1862...
Snickers Gap, Va., October 27th, 1862..
Philamount, Va, November 1st, 1862..
Union, Va., November 2d, 1862.........
Upperville, Va., November 3d, 1862....
Barber's Cross Roads, Va., November 5th, 1862.....................................
Amosville, Va., November 7th—12th, 1962.....................................
Jefferson, Va., November 13th, 1862...
Sulphur Springs, Va. Novemper 15th, 1862.....................................
Skirmish, Freemans Ford, Va., April 11th, 1863.....................................
Skirmish, Beverly Ford, Va., April 14th, 1863.....................................
Skirmish, Kelleys Ford, Va., April 29th, 1863.....................................
Skirmish, Rapidan, Va., May 1st, 1863
Chancellorsville, Va. May 2nd—4th, 1863.....................................
Beverly Ford, Va., June 9th, 1863......
Middleburg and Upperville, Va., June 14th, 1863.....................................
Gettysburg, Pa., July 1st—4th, 1863...
Williamsport, Md., July 6th, 1863......
Boonsboro, Md. July 8th, 1863.........
Funkestown, Md. July 9th, 1863......
Falling Waters, Md., July 12th, 1863..
Brandy Station, Va., August 1st—4th, 1863.....................................
Culpepper, Va., September 13th, 1863..
Raccoon Ford, Va., September 14th, 1863.....................................
Germania Ford, Va., October 10th, 1863.....................................
Stevansburg, Va., October 11th, 1863..
Oak Hill, Va., October 15th, 1863......
Bealton Station, Va., November 2nd, 1863.....................................
Culpepper, Va., November 8th, 1863...
Skirmish, Hesiers Gap, Va., July 18th, 1863.....................................
Skirmish, Brandy Station, Va., October 12th, 1863.....................................
Skirmish, Barnet Ford, Va., February 6th—7th, 1863.....................................
Craig's Meeting House, Va., May 5th. 1864.....................................
Spottsylvania Court House, Va., May 8th, 1864.....................................
Yellow Tavern, Va., May 11th. 1864....
Meadow Bridge, Va., May 12th, 1864...
Hanover Court House, Va., May 31st, 1864.....................................
Haines Shop, Va., June 3d, 1864.......
White Oak Swamp, Va., June 13th, 1864.....................................
Malvern Hill, Va., June 15th, 1864.....
Nottoway Court House, Va., June 23d,
Roanoake Station, Va., June 25th, 1864.....................................
Stony Creek, Va., June 28th, 1864......
Reams Station, Va., June 29th, 1864...
Winchester, Va., August 17th, 1864....
Kearneystown, Va., August 25th, 1864..
Winchester, Va., September 19th, 1864
Front Royal, Va., September 21st, 1864.....................................
Tom's Brook, Va., October 9th, 1864...
Cedar Creek, Va., October, 19th, 1864..
Middletown, Va., November 12th, 1864
Lacy Springs, Va., December 21st, 1864.....................................
Gordonsville, Va., December 23d, 1864..
Waynesboro, Va., March 2nd, 1865. ...
Beaver Dam Station, Va., March 13th, 1865.....................................
North Anna Bridge, Va., March 14th, 1865.....................................
Five Points, Va., April 1st, 1865........
Scotts Corners, Va., April 2d, 1865.....
Dinwiddie Court House, Va., March 31st, 1865.....................................
Sweet House Creek, Va., April 3d, 1865
Amelia Court House, Va, April 4th—5th, 1865.....................................
Sailors Creek, Va., April 6th, 1865....
Appomattox Station, Va., April 8th, 1885.....................................

ADDENDA.

The following communications were received too late for publication in their proper places in this book, but as they are of interest to every reader the author deems it best that they be published in this addenda form:

OUR NEW MAJOR GENERAL.

[From an Oregon Paper.]

HUNTINGTON, Or., Feb. 27th, 1887.

Col. H. B. Compson, of this place, recently appointed Major-General of the Oregon State militia by Governor Pennoyer, was born in Seneca County, N. Y., in 1844. He enlisted as a private soldier in the War of the Rebellion at the age of 17, in the Eighth New York Cavalry. Before the close of the war he had filled every office in the regiment, through a continuous line of promotion from Corporal to Colonel, each promotion being made by reason of meritorious service and gallant conduct upon the battlefield.

He was twice wounded, and four horses were shot under him. He was with Colonel Davis's command, under General Miles, that cut its way out of Harper's Ferry when surrounded by General Jackson's forces—Miles surrendered to Jackson next day—and upon this occasion captured from the enemy 125 wagons loaded with ammunition. He was in command of the advance regiments at the battle of

Waynesborough, Va.,—General Sheridan, Corps Commander—and was ordered by General Custer to charge the enemy that day in his stronghold, against the destructive fire of six pieces of artillery planted in his face.

This gallant charge, which resulted in the capture of the six pieces of artillery, 1,350 prisoners, 250 wagons and ambulances, 1,500 stand of arms, 1,200 horses, 6 forges and 17 battle-flags, called from Sheridan and Custer personal compliments upon the field, and Sheridan detailed Colonel Compson to convey the captured flags, together with dispatches, to Washington. On account of his gallant services that day he was voted a medal of honor by Congress and was commissioned Brevet-Colonel by Secretary Stanton, and promoted to full Colonelcy by the Governor of New York.

The records of the battles of Antietam, Harper's Ferry, Gettysburg, Winchester, Cedar Creek, of Sheridan's raid, of Wilson's raid, the battle of Five Forks and the surrender of General Lee at Appomattox show that Colonel Compson took an active part in the great struggle for the preservation of the Union, from the opening till the close of the war. He was a brave and gallant soldier, and in every way deserves the honor which Governor Pennoyer has conferred.

Hartwell B. Compson was born in the town of Tyre, Seneca County, New York, May 4th, 1844, was a farmer until the breaking out of war, not being of age could not get his parents' consent to enlist, had to run away, and enlisted in Captain B. F. Sisson's Company G, September 28th, 1861, at Seneca Falls, N. Y., same day joined the regiment at Rochester; was appointed Corporal October 1st, 1861; Sergeant, October 10th, 1861; First Sergeant, December 8th, 1862; promoted to Second Lieutenant, August 29th, 1862;

First Lieutenant, August 14th, 1863; Captain, February 9th, 1864; Major, December 7th, 1864; Brevet Lieutenant-Colonel, February 28th, 1865; Brevet-Colonel, March 2d, 1865; was in command of the regiment from February 28th, 1865, on Sheridan's raid from Winchester to White House Landing.

Colonel H. B. Compson, of Klamath Agency, Klamath County, Oregon, is wearing to-day a medal of honor presented by Congress for accomplishing the greatest feat during the rebellion, the great charge of the Eighth New York Cavalry at Waynesboro, Va., March 2d, 1865.

CONGRATULATORY ORDER FROM GENERAL CUSTER.

The following congratulatory order has been issued by General Custer to the men and officers of the Third Division of the Cavalry Corps. The praise given has been fairly won by the bravery, courage and determination of the division in the recent engagements in the Valley:

HEADQUARTERS THIRD DIVISION, CAVALRY CORPS, M. M. D.
October 21st, 1864.

Soldiers of the Third Cavalry Division:

With pride and gratification your Commanding General congratulates you upon your brilliant achievements of the past few days.

On the 9th of the present month you attacked a vastly superior force of the enemy's cavalry, strongly posted with artillery in position, and commanded by that famous "Savior of the Valley," Rosser.

Notwithstanding the enemy's superiority in numbers and position, you drove him twenty miles, capturing his artillery—six pieces in all; also his entire train of wagons and ambulances, and a large number of prisoners. Again, during the memorable engagement of the 19th instant, your conduct throughout was sublimely heroic, and without a parallel in the annals of warfare. In the early part of the day, when disaster and defeat seemed to threaten our noble army upon all sides, your calm and determined bearing, while exposed to a terrible fire from the enemy's guns, added not a little to restore confidence to that portion of our army already broken and driven back on the right.

Afterwards, rapidly transferred from the right flank to the extreme left, you materially and successfully assisted in defeating the enemy in his attempt to turn the left flank of our army.

Again, ordered on the right flank, you attacked and defeated a division of the enemy's cavalry, driving him in confusion across Cedar Creek.

Then changing your front to the left at a gallop, you charged and turned the left flank of the enemy's line of battle, and pursued his broken and demoralized army a distance of five miles.

Night alone put an end to your pursuit. Among the substantial fruits of this great victory, you can boast of having captured five battle-flags, a large number of prisoners, including Major General Ramseur, and forty-five of the forty-eight pieces of artillery taken from the enemy on that day—thus making fifty-one pieces of artillery which you have captured from the enemy within the short period of ten days.

This is a record of which you may well be proud —a record won and established by your gallantry and perseverance.

You have surrounded the name of the Third Cavalry Division with a halo as enduring as time.

The history of this war, when truthfully written, will contain no brighter page than that upon which is recorded the chivalrous deeds, the glorious triumphs of the soldiers of the Third Division.

C. A. CUSTER,
Brigadier General Commanding.

Official—CHAS. SIEBERT, Captain and A. A. Gen'l.

ERRATA.

Page 28—"roads" should read woods.
Page 64—"June 28th" should read June 8th.
Page 86—"disbanded" should read disembarked.
Page 123—"Third Corps" should read different corps.

www.ingramcontent.com/pod-product-compliance
Lightning Source LLC
Chambersburg PA
CBHW031440160426
43195CB00010BB/795